# Examining the Beloved Disciple

From the River Jordan to the Island of Patmos

## Jason Lee Willis

Lura Publications

Mapleton, MN

**Lura Publications**
**803 Silver Street E.**
**Mapleton, MN 56065**
**www.lurapublications.wixsite.com/books**
**williswrites.com**

Book Layout © 2017 BookDesignTemplates.com

**Examining the Beloved Disciple/ Jason Lee Willis**. – 2nd ed.
ISBN 979-8-9903790-6-0

This one is dedicated to John.
Not THE John (St. John, the Beloved Disciple, etc.)
This one is dedicated to "Big" John, who not only steers my
canoe while I paddle like a madman but also steers my
research topics.

# Contents

# QUITE THE TRIP

So when your wife is a travel agent, and you are a teacher, there are countless opportunities to travel during the summer if you pinch your pennies. A typical English teacher might request a trip to the Globe Theater in England, Walden Pond, or Hannibal, Missouri. An English teacher who moonlights as a Bible Study teacher might want to go to Rome, Egypt, or the most obvious destination...Israel.

How about Patmos, honey?

(Patmos is literally a big rock in the Mediterranean Sea.)

Or Ephesus?

You know, the center of one of the largest pagan shrines in antiquity, the Sin City of its day where hardly anything Biblical happened!

Somehow, I convinced her to book this trip, not as a research opportunity to help me write this book you're holding in your hands but to scratch an itch.

What was itching?

Before reading this, you must first understand that I have an irrational faith. I have a very BIG God and as a result, I always look for the most EPIC interpretation possible instead of trying to find a safe, reasonable interpretation that makes it as palpable to the masses as possible. Also, I'm not going to out-research anybody or try to convince you to join a cult or begin a new Christian denomination. Although I'd like to remain a generic "Christian," we all know that many flags fly in the name of Christ, so I'll declare it right now: I'm a Luth-o-lic-a-tist (my flag is a mess). My secret agenda is only to make you go...huh.

Early in my personal study of scripture, there would be several passages involving St. John that stopped me in my tracks, and when I turned to conventional scholarship for answers, my wrinkled brow would reach Shar Pei levels.

But..but...but…

Many of my answers were found outside, under, and next to the box, so yes, this study of John will get a bit EPIC. I'm sure you'll be able to find your own scholar to support your own existing beliefs, but remember this: the scholars in Jesus's (English teacher rule=I added a syllable to Jesus and since an apostrophe does not make noise, I added the s for the double S sound. Gee-Sus-es) time were so rigid that only open-minded simple folks recognized the truth. Yes, I could be wrong on a whole bunch of stuff, but I'm just asking you to keep an open mind. Once again, the noise you need to make is….huh. Let's avoid angry WHAT!!!!!

Oh, the itch? The only apostle to die in the context of the Bible is James (excluding Judas Iscariot, of course), leaving TRADITION to give us a wild ride of various accounts, many of which are quite horrible (See Chapter 5), with only the man of the hour, John, dying of old age. This is when my wrinkled forehead went from Shar Pei level of confusion to full on transparent mode that allowed the wrinkles of my own brain to be seen as they pulsed with confusion over some EPIC verses that contradicted tradition.

So, I booked a trip and stood in Ephesus at the place claiming to be the resting place of St. John—to scratch an itch. And as I stood there metaphorically scratching that itch, I knew I had to share my theory with my Bible study groups back in Minnesota, and now, with you also.

While you certainly can glean the direction I'm going by glancing at my Table of Contents, I'll give you the spoiler right now: John will be one of the Two Witnesses.

There, I said it.

I'm not sure if your forehead is smooth, wrinkled, Shar Pei, or transparent skull right now, but even if I fail to convince you, John is an AWESOME apostle to study, so I hope you can stay with me and flip the next page.

J.L.W.

# CHAPTER ONE

# THE SONS OF THUNDER

## John is so Cool

Seriously, this guy is THE MAN. Even when he messes up (and he does), his mistakes tend to be epic and awesome instead of shameful (like Peter). This entire book is dedicated to understanding him better as a person and instrument of righteousness, so we're going to start with a study of his family and how he got such a cool nickname...the Son of Thunder.

Okay, James was also a Son of Thunder, but this book isn't about him, is it? He got all the glory being the firstborn son of Zebedee, and now, it's time to put the spotlight on his kid brother.

The nickname comes from Mark, and only there, which is interesting since Mark himself was not an initial disciple. To me, this means the nickname spread after the years of Jesus's ministry. I'll be using the old English KJV not because it's the best but because I like to show how English words can change meaning, which will prompt us to look at what the original texts said. For example, if I asked my English students to give me a synonym for the word "pretty," we could go around the whole room with a different word. Translations can be like that also since the translator can try to pick the best English word to match the original text.

**[Mark 3:17] And James the son of Zebedee, and John the brother of James; and he surnamed them Boanerges, which is, The sons of thunder:**

See, even Mark leads with James, and John is almost the afterthought. Although the HE isn't capitalized to indicate Jesus, it is Jesus who surnamed them. How awesome is that? Jesus rebrands them as the Sons of Thunder. BOANERGES!!!

I'd wear the title with pride.

But why did Jesus give them that phrase? It doesn't really explain, which leads to speculation, which fuels this whole book. Notice that folks like Mark identified them first as the sons of Zebedee (I'll get to him in a bit). The word BOANERGES and BRONTES are literally meant to mean thunder and figuratively commotion. So is it characterizing their dad or does it reflect on their personality?

Assuming it is meant to describe them, it is Jesus who names them this early in his ministries, so is his use of it after gaining first impressions of the boys, or being prophetic, does he give them the name knowing what James and (especially) John will be like in their future?

Regardless, it's a pretty sweet nickname (better than "rock").

# Mr. Zebedee

There are a dozen or so references to the man named Zebedee, but nearly all of them are in reference to the "sons of Zebedee." That in itself says a lot when contrasting it to the way the other disciples are introduced. We can infer that Zebedee is KNOWN. I'm not saying that he's famous, but either the Galileans or early Christians knew who he was and what he was all about. For all four Gospel writers to bring up James and John in connection to their dad means something, doesn't it?

If you use the metaphor of the "apple doesn't fall far from the tree," then the assumption could be that if your sons are special enough to become disciples of Jesus, then YOU must have done a good job raising them. There is some strong logic in this claim.

Luckily, we do have an actual Zebedee sighting in the Gospels that lets us explore the father of John a bit more. It's not much, but it does support a few conclusions. Let's look:

> **[Matthew 4:18] And Jesus, walking by the sea of Galilee, saw two brethren, Simon called Peter, and Andrew his brother, casting a net into the sea: for they were fishers. [19] And he saith unto them, Follow me, and I will make you fishers of men. [20] And they straightway left their nets, and followed him. [21] And going on from thence, he saw other two brethren, James the son of Zebedee, and John his brother, in a ship with Zebedee their father, mending their nets; and he called them. [22] And they immediately left the ship and their father, and followed him.**

First, let's talk about the context and chronology of this moment. It is NOT the first time Jesus has seen James and John. Many preachers, reading Matthew first, often think this is the first time, but if you read The Gospel of John, you'll realize that Jesus met the Sons of Thunder previously when he was in Judea (at the baptism scene). According to John (who knows better than Matthew), he met Jesus during the baptism scene, along with Andrew, and they went from being disciples of the Baptist and became disciples of the Christ. Jesus brought them home to Galilee, and after a wedding, went out into the Wilderness to confront Satan.

Since I had to make sense of the sequence of events, I've come to see this as Jesus going to Jerusalem for the Feast of Dedication (December) when he bumps into the Baptist, add a week of travel to get to Galilee, then at least forty days in the Wilderness (possibly getting back as well). If you line up all the verses, it seems to me that Jesus returned to Judea around the time of Passover, and THEN he went back to Galilee. So it's been approximately three months since John has seen Jesus when Jesus returns for Matthew 4:18.

Okay, back to Zebedee.

Now, John the Baptist has already handed off John and Andrew to Jesus, but this scene officially adds the older brothers to the gang.

Did you picture Jesus alone on the shore?

It's doubtful he's alone.

According to John (Chapter 2:13-4:54), before Jesus showed up for this scene, he went to Judea, where he met Nicodemus for the first time, confronted the moneychangers for the first time, stops in Samaria (which was on the way), arrives in Galilee, heals a nobleman's son, and THEN returns to Sea of Galilee. In the context of all of that, it mentions Jesus picking up disciples, which would mean he brought his Judean disciples (John 2:17) to join up with his Galilean crew of Matthew 4:18.

This stuff matters to me, okay.

Yes, now it's really time for Zebedee.

**Mark 1:20** says pretty much the same thing with one verse that adds more **And straightway he called them: and they left their father Zebedee in the ship with the hired servants, and went after him.** So Zebedee has servants along with his sons. While wealth is relative, Zebedee is not living hand to mouth. He can hire servants to help with his fishing operation. According to tradition, Simon Peter had a wife and was also an oldest son (of Jonah). If Zebedee is the boss, then **Luke** adds an interesting fact in **5:10**. Now, the context of Luke's verse is several months later in the fall, and when Jesus vanishes, Peter goes right back to work instead of waiting for Jesus. **And so was also James, and John, the sons of Zebedee, which were partners with Simon. And Jesus said unto Simon, Fear not; from henceforth thou shalt catch men.** Jesus is calling out Peter for getting "worldly" again. This shows that he is a "partner" with the Zebedee operation. See him as a manager for the fleet. He's Zebedee's right hand man, which was why he went back to the business (only to get chided by Jesus).

This builds on the idea that Zebedee has quite an operation, leading me to realize that folks knew him because he fed Galilee. He's the McZebedee of Galilee.

Why is this important?

James, as firstborn son, is destined to own the family business one day when Zebedee retires. Simon Peter is being groomed to "run" the operation for James, which is why he is seen as a partner. I don't know if Jonah is a fisherman too, or if Zebedee hired Simon Peter, who is working his way up the ladder of the business. Jonah could be a carpenter for all I know. McZebedee, however, has clout and money. What does he do with his money?

He invests it in John.

John?

The role of a second son means you don't get jack squat. Your brother inherits the business. If you're on good terms, you can work for him. If not, well, learn a new trade. When we first meet John, it is found in his own Gospel,

> **[John 1:35] Again the next day after John stood, and <u>two of his</u> <u>disciples</u>; [36] And looking upon Jesus as he walked, he saith, Behold the Lamb of God! [37] And <u>the two disciples</u> heard him speak, and <u>they followed Jesus</u>. [38] Then Jesus turned, and saw them following, and saith unto them, What seek ye? They said unto him, Rabbi, (which is to say, being interpreted, Master,) where dwellest thou? [39] He saith unto them, Come and see. They came and saw where he dwelt, and abode with him that day: for it was about the tenth hour. [40] <u>One of the</u> <u>two which heard John speak, and followed him, was Andrew</u>, Simon Peter's brother.**

Okay, so if one of the Baptist's disciples was Andrew, the other was...the author, John. My point is that Zebedee sent his second son to be trained and taught by JOHN THE BAPTIST, the most famous preacher and prophet of the time. He didn't send him to some lousy local Pharisee, or even to an awesome Pharisee like Nicodemus. He sent him to the Baptist. How does John live day to day when his mentor is eating bugs? Zebedee supported John's liberal arts education. Zebedee recognized the authority and righteousness of the Baptist, which says volumes about his own faith and intuition.

## Appositively NOT Aunt Mary

Not only do we learn the identity of the father of James and John, we also learn a bit about their mother. Now I have to warn you, after the first anecdote, I'm going to get off track a bit when discussing the most popular name in the Gospels—Mary.

First, let's meet Mom.

**[Matthew 20:20] Then came to him the mother of Zebedee's children with her sons, worshipping him, and desiring a certain thing of him. [21] And he said unto her, What wilt thou? She saith unto him, Grant that these my two sons may sit, the one on thy right hand, and the other on the left, in thy kingdom. [22] But Jesus answered and said, Ye know not what ye ask. Are ye able to drink of the cup that I shall drink of, and to be baptized with the baptism that I am baptized with? They say unto him, We are able. [23] And he saith unto them, Ye shall drink indeed of my cup, and be baptized with the baptism that I am baptized with: but to sit on my right hand, and on my left, is not mine to give, but it shall be given to them for whom it is prepared of my Father.**

**[24] And when the ten heard it, they were moved with indignation against the two brethren. [25] But Jesus called them unto him, and said, Ye know that the princes of the Gentiles exercise dominion over them, and they that are great**

**exercise authority upon them. [26] But it shall not be so among you: but whosoever will be great among you, let him be your minister; [27] And whosoever will be chief among you, let him be your servant: [28] Even as the Son of man came not to be ministered unto, but to minister, and to give his life a ransom for many.**

Okay, so there is a ton of stuff going on in the passage that needs to be unpacked. In the sequence of things, this anecdote seems to happen in the final year and more likely than not, the last trip to Jerusalem for the Passover. While this could indicate that Jesus had a large convoy, it might also mean it was a convoy of convenience since most Jews traveled for Passover. Seeing Mrs. Zebedee in the crowd is nothing too abnormal, but she definitely seems to understand this lamb is being led to slaughter. Then she offers up her own lambs. Dang, mom!

Mark 10 clarifies this scene, and removes Mrs. Zebedee from the same question. Did somebody make a mistake? In reading this scene, all you need to do is picture a throng of people, with Mrs. Z, James, and John all in close proximity.

"Go ask him."

"Now?"

"If you don't, I'll ask him."

"Right…"

"Hey Jesus, Grant that my sons…"

"What is she doing?"

James pushes his mother to the side and continues, "Grant that we might…"

Mashing these two scenes together makes Mrs. Zebedee certainly seem like an advocate for her sons and a woman who understands the concept and purpose of the Christ as a sacrificial lamb. Since this chapter will also discuss James, we'll get back to the request in just a bit. I want to spend a few minutes exploring the relationship of Mrs. Z as a follower of Christ.

Again, everybody and their mother (see what I did there) were going to Jerusalem for the Passover, so it's hard to determine if Mrs. Z stayed with or not. However, I've come across a lot of speculation about the whole Zebedee clan that doesn't make sense to me (the cousins theory). The root of this problem is found in the lists of WHO was at the CROSS.

First, let's talk about all the guys who were at the cross.

John.

Yes, John was the only disciple to get to witness the crucifixion (I'll explain in the next chapter). The rest of the "pro-Jesus" crowd were the Galilean women, the Mourners-R-Us club, and the startled folks passing by for the Passover.

For good or bad, the Gospel writers listed out these women.

John, who was a witness and wrote his account AFTER the other three, had this to say:

**[John 19:25] Now there stood by the cross of Jesus his mother, and his mother's sister, Mary the wife of Cleophas, and Mary Magdalene. [26] When Jesus therefore saw his mother, and the disciple standing by, whom he loved, he saith unto his mother, Woman, behold thy son! [27] Then saith he to the disciple, Behold thy mother! And from that hour that disciple took her unto his own home.**

So the Cousin Theory is that Jesus is related to James and John through their mothers. This is based on a quick reading of the above text as well as the other Gospel writers. As an English teacher, I see kids struggle with the use of commas in lists all the time. Look at verse 25 and tell me how many people you see?

1. Mother Mary?
2. His mother's sister?
3. Mary the wife of Cleophas (now spelled Clopas to avoid confusion with Peter)
4. Mary Magdalene.

Four, sir! In just a bit, I'll drop more details about woman #2 and how people have connected it, but since we're talking about appositive phrases, phrases that give detail to the subject (like this one), I want you to open your minds to the fact that John listed off 3 women.

1. Mother Mary
2. Aunt Mary, the wife of Clopas
3. Mary Magdalene.

See it now...three Marys. How do you tell them apart if you are John? You add an appositive phrase. Which Mary? The Wife of Clopas. If you've read my Examining Christmas book, you know I believe Clopas was the brother of Joseph. His wife Mary was "sister-in-law" to the Virgin Mary. When Clopas died, care for his wife and children went to Joseph (or possibly the other way around). There are verses that list out the brothers of Jesus (named James, Jude, Simon, and Joses). My Uncle Clopas theory preserves the sanctity of the Virgin Mary's womb while also explaining how a cousin became a brother. That is why John clarified that the second Mary BESIDE HIM at the cross was the woman known as Mrs. Clopas to others, sister-in-law to the Virgin Mary, and Aunt Mary to Jesus.

I do find it strange that John doesn't reference his OWN mother in this account, since Matthew (who wasn't there) listed her as being a witness at the cross. The Matthew account is what fuels the Cousin Theory. The fact that Mrs. Zebedee is there makes the context of the anecdote strange. Jesus looks down from the cross to the two most emotionally raw people witnessing the execution. He gives John to the Virgin Mary, and then he gives the Virgin Mary to John.

What the heck?

Remember, according to Matthew, John's mother is right there. Weird? Uncomfortable for her? Plus, we've already established that Jesus had real brothers/cousins NOT named John who could have taken care of his mother. The Virgin Mary had caretakers. So the purpose of Jesus connecting John and Mother Mary was not pragmatic—it was spiritual (we'll get to that later).

Let's get things really muddy by bringing up the other Gospel accounts.

> **[Mark 15:40] There were also women looking on afar off: among whom was Mary Magdalene, and Mary the mother of James the less and of Joses, and Salome.**

And

> **[Matt 27:56]: Among them were Mary Magdalene, Mary the mother of James and Joseph, and the mother of Zebedee's sons.**

And Luke's list from the Easter morning scene:

> **[Luke 24:10] It was Mary Magdalene, and Joanna, and Mary the mother of James, and other women that were with them, which told these things unto the apostles.**

Confused?

Let's start again with the most women possible

1. The Virgin Mary.
2. Mary's sister
3. Mary Magdalene.
4. The Mother of James and Joseph was there
5. The Wife of Clopas
6. Mrs. Zebedee
7. Salome.
8. Possibly Joanna
9. Other woman

The Cousin Theory tries to merge multiple Jameses into one James. Again, in my Uncle Clopas theory, I let cousins=brothers work based on traditional Hebrew customs. Plus, here is the list one more time:

Matt 13:55: Brothers=James, Joses, Simon, and Jude

Mark 3:31: Brothers

Matt 12:46: Brothers

Luke 8:19: Brothers

John 7: Brothers


Here is how I see the lists coming together:

1. The Virgin Mary
2. Mary Magdalene
3. Aunt Mary, the Wife of Clopas, Sister-in-Law to Mary, mother of 4 boys (J,J,S,J)
4. Mrs. Zebedee, who might be named Salome (or even Joanna)

Three Marys, yes, but then again, there are three Jameses as well.

# Just 1 James? Sorry.

While we're on the subject of Uncle Clopas/Aunt Mary, let's talk about those brother-cousins of Jesus. If you read the above verses, Jesus separated his disciples from his brothers, and when you read John 7, you realize why. The brother-cousins seemed jealous and envious (if not scheming). The four children listed as brother-cousins were James, Joses, Simon, and Jude (with spelling variations).

**James Alphaeus.** James, the son of Alphaeus, is Disciple #9 in my list. Since Jesus has both Galilean and Judean disciples, I assume he is possibly one of the Judean disciples he picked up in Jerusalem after the trip to the Wilderness. Tradition says he died in Egypt. That James.

James Alphaeus was with Jesus when Jesus made the distinction between his family and his flock. Not a brother. Total disciple.

**James the Son of Zebedee**, aka a Son of Thunder, is the other disciple named James. He is Disciple #2/#3 in the disciple list, depending on who you read. Clearly Galilean. Clearly the brother of John. Clearly the son of Zebedee. His mom's name? Not clear. His death? Crystal clear (we'll finish with that).

**James the Just** is the brother-cousin of Jesus. He's the one that Jesus dismisses in favor of his disciples. He's the Son of Clopas. His mother is most likely named Mary (but not THE Mary). He prodded Jesus into going to Jerusalem to "reveal himself" (it was most likely a trap). As a brother-cousin, raised by two Marys, this guy knows his stuff but has some major issues also, keeping him separate from being a disciple. Take a look at Paul's reference to him:

**[1 Corinthians 15:3] For I delivered unto you first of all that which I also received, how that Christ died for our sins according to the scriptures; [4] And that he was buried, and that he rose again the third day according to the scriptures: [5] And that he was seen of Cephas, then of the twelve: [6] After that, he was seen of above five hundred brethren at once; of whom the greater part remain unto this present, but some are fallen asleep. [7] After that, he was seen of James; then of all the apostles. [8] And last of all he was seen of me also, as of one born out of due time. [9] For I am the least of the apostles, that am not meet to be called an apostle, because I persecuted the church of God.**

A.   Jesus died, got it.

B.   Seen by Simon Peter "The Rock," yep, right after the Road to Emmaus

C.   The 12. Yep (I won't quibble Thomas/Judas)

D.   500 brethren. Sure, during those 40 days.

E.   James...

F.   The Apostles, sure, when he ascended.

Wait! Which James is E? Hold on, didn't James Z and James A see him in event C and event F. Whoa...brother-cousin Jesus needed a moment, didn't he? James the Son of Clopas needed to be "restored" just like Simon Peter. Wow, who is this guy?

James Clopas is easy to distinguish in the Book of Acts. You see, James Zebebee is beheaded in 12:2, and then later, another James is mentioned in Acts 12:17 "Go tell James and the Brethren" and again in Acts 14, when Peter and Paul debate whether Christians need to be Jews first. To settle the matter, they go to an independent source...James Clopas. Even later, Jude (the other brother-cousin) references his brother in Jude 1:1. Galatians 1:19 references "James, the Lord's brother."

Historically, James Clopas becomes known as "**James the Just**" or "James the Righteous" because of his vital role in early Christianity. As seen in Acts 14, THIS James is a double-agent of sorts. After being "restored" by Jesus in a private moment, James the Just becomes scriptural authority for Paul and Peter. According to Eusebius, James the Just was one of the most trusted men in Judaism also, right up until the Pharisees murdered him when he took a stand for Christians during Passover/Easter. He was a cool dude. (I believe) This is the same guy who is labeled by Mark as James the Less:

> **[Mark 15:40] There were also women looking on afar off: among whom was Mary Magdalene, and Mary the mother of James the less and of Joses, and Salome;**

I've heard theories that James the Less is James Alphaeus, you know, uncool James. However, this is NOT what Mark meant when he wrote "the less." The word in Greek is Omikros, which I first came across when reading the Iliad to distinguish Big Ajax (the hero) and Little Ajax (the rapist). So Mark is trying to distinguish which of the 3 Jameses by calling this one "little James."

James Zebedee...James Alphaeus...James Clopas

Yet for James Thunderson, err...James Zebedee, there is a major obstacle to me loosely accepting him as a cousin for Jesus. I understand how scholars try to connect Matthew and Mark's account and FORCE Mrs. Zebedee into being the mother of James, Joses, Simon, and Jude. But what about John? So lining up the names from the two lists does NOT PROVE anything, but I believe logic helps clarify why I do not think James and John could have been cousins of Jesus.

> **[John 1:40] One of the two which heard John** (the Baptist) **speak, and followed him, was Andrew, Simon Peter's brother. [41] He first findeth his own brother Simon, and saith unto him, We have found the Messias, which is, being interpreted, the Christ. [42] And he brought him to Jesus. And when Jesus beheld him, he said, Thou art Simon the son of Jona: thou shalt be called Cephas, which is by interpretation, A stone.**

Okay, now you have to remember that the OTHER apprentice of the Baptist was John Zebedee. He's there also. So when Andrew declares "WE" have found the Messiah, he's speaking with John right by him. Not only does it seem as if there has been an APB for the Christ, but that Peter has been looking too. So when they find Jesus, they run and tell Peter, and later James.

Hold on, if Jesus was a COUSIN from GALILEE, are you saying the Sons of Thunder NEVER bumped into Jesus before? This is where the logic and premise of Jesus being cousins to the Thunderson boys wears thin. There is genuine surprise and joy at finding the lost Christ child last seen heading south to Egypt.

Okay, so now that we've met Zebedee, Mrs. Z (not a Mary), and his big brother James (not Alphaeus or Omikros), I'm ready to introduce you to our shining star himself, John Boy.

# CHAPTER TWO

# LITTLE JOHN
# (oo-de-lally)

So how do you end up with a moniker of "The Beloved Disciple" when Jesus is the type of global savior that, you know, treats everybody equally?

A.  Big Ego
B.  The other disciples were lame
C.  You're just that awesome
D.  A cool plan for you in the End Times
E.  Other

To fairly answer that question, we're going to have to do some deep digging into the story of John. With me, you'll usually get a few possible answers to choose from, and of course, I'll try to make all of them work with an "all of the above" twist. Since we finished talking about the family of John, I'd like to spend some time talking about the disciple we see in the context of the gospels. My assumption is that you already have some familiarity with John, so I'm going to jump right into a theory of mine and then support it with an overview of anecdotes. Ready?

John was a kid.

## Exhibit A: The Lean

Seriously, forget all about that bearded disciple with thinning hair and one of those full-length tunics. John is an all elbows-and-knees teenager. He has no responsibilities or obligations (unlike the other disciples) and can be there day or night at Jesus's side. Let's start with the most awkward bit of evidence.

[**John 21:20 Then Peter, turning about, seeth the disciple whom Jesus loved following; which also leaned on his breast at supper,**]

There is a WHOLE LOT I want to talk about in Chapter 21, but I'll save that for later. I want to focus on the origin of the "Beloved Disciple" moniker here, which is written by the guy who is being talked about. Yes, John is referencing himself without saying ME, ME, ME. There is a strange humility in the entire Gospel of John we'll discuss later. In this anecdote, Peter is being restored, and he brings up John, but it is John who brings up a very strange detail—he leaned on Jesus during the last supper.

Can you imagine a forty-year-old Peter cuddling up next to Jesus and putting his head on Jesus's chest during the late hours of the Passover Ritual?

Okay, Jesus likes to cuddle. Think about cuddling with your mama and then compare that to your Messiah. Sure, Jesus could like to cuddle. Mentally filming this scene with a bearded, bald man is a bit unusual considering the reverence given to the ceremony.

Yet, if John was a fifteen-year-old Hebrew kid, the whole mentor-mentee relationship works a lot better. Jesus does not "love" John more than the other disciples because John is better than any of them; Jesus "loves" John because he's just a kid.

Remember when Mark wrote,

**[Mark 10:14] But when Jesus saw it, he was much displeased, and said unto them, Suffer the little children to come unto me, and forbid them not: for of such is the kingdom of God.**

Not only would a young evangelist like Mark notice this about Jesus, I think the behavior would transfer onto the youngest disciple, John.

## Exhibit B: The Baptist's Apprentice

While there is nothing definitive in this argument, the concept of being an apprentice is pretty basic. If a blacksmith is reputable, and you want your son to learn a trade, you send him to be the apprentice of the blacksmith. While your kid is free of responsibility, he can learn the ropes while also providing a free service to the blacksmith.

Now compare this to the John the Baptist situation. Since John the Elijah was born (seriously, if you don't know the JB=E theory, order my *Examining Christmas* book), folks have known the guy was special. I believe he was smuggled out of Judea as a child and grew up "in the wilderness" which can be a reference to the wilderness between Judea and Babylon (then Parthia). When John the Baptist returns to Judea, he already seems famous enough to warrant the attention of royalty and the Pharisees of the day. He also must have been seen as a spiritual authority. Why do I say that? He had disciples.

Do you hear about Nicodemus having a posse? Or Joseph of Arimathea having a crew? Nope, but John the Baptist has a large enough following that even when it is gleaned by Jesus, he still has other disciples that remain with him to run messages back and forth to Jesus. I don't want to get off topic with the baptism scene, so I'm pulling out a few key moments that pertain to John Zebedee.

> **[John 1:15] John bare witness of him, and cried, saying, This was he of whom I spake, He that cometh after me is preferred before me: for he was before me.**

(Obviously, John has talked to his crew about the pending arrival of the Christ).

> **[John 1:23] He said, I am the voice of one crying in the wilderness, Make straight the way of the Lord, as said the prophet Esaias.**

(Have you ever pondered what "making straight the way" means? After all, the Baptist seems to be a flash in the pan. How did he prepare things for Christ? Unless…)

> **[John 1:29] The next day John seeth Jesus coming unto him, and saith, Behold the Lamb of God, which taketh away the sin of the world. [30] This is he of whom I said, After me cometh a man which is preferred before me: for he was before me.**

(Again, John is not only excited about being able to see the Christ since he was in utero, but he's also excited about his part in the story: PREPARATION.)

**[John 1:35] Again the next day after John stood, and two of his disciples; [36] And looking upon Jesus as he walked, he saith, Behold the Lamb of God! [37] And the two disciples heard him speak, and they followed Jesus.**

(And there it is! John the Baptist is the quarterback handing the ball to the running back. He's been "preparing the way" yet the only act we have is that he has two disciples he's been specifically training for this day.)

Those two disciples mentioned are Andrew and the unnamed John. I'd like to take this moment to offer a theory on why John Zebedee refuses to name himself in the story or use a first person pronoun like I or Me. If you read the entirety of John chapter one, you'll see the reverence JZ has for JB. Keep in mind, JB is 30 years old, and if JZ is only 13 here, then when Zebedee names his baby, it is possible that a famous 17-year-old JB could already be preaching in the Wilderness. What if he is named John in tribute to the Baptist? OR...it is a coincidence, but it's like being born with the name Jesus Jones a year before Jesus became famous. Are you worthy of the name Jesus? Nope. Time for a new name. So it is possible that the apprentice feels unworthy (Wayne's World Thought Bubble) in comparison to his master.

Being the apprentice of JB means you've had some unworldly knowledge and training, which is why the big four (hey, let's step aside for some Jesus talk) always seem to be James & John and Andrew & Peter. Two of these four were trained by JB. How's that for a pedigree! While it is possible to throw a marriage and family to the wind to become an apprentice, it traditionally makes sense for a young man to do so.

# Exhibit C: Entrance to the Trial

There is another peculiar moment that left me scratching my head. Do you remember how Peter denied Jesus three times while warming his hands at a burn barrel (hmm? Or was that something I saw in a play). Anyway, Jesus was hauled before a kangaroo court in the middle of the night, where the bad guys could quickly convict him while everybody else was sleeping-in following a long night during the Passover Ritual. By the time they woke up, Jesus was supposed to be nailed to the cross. It was an evil and efficient plan.

Yet in all of those details, it is easy to forget that John went with Peter to check on the trial. Let's take a closer look:

> **[Matthew 26:36] Then cometh Jesus with them unto a place called Gethsemane, and saith unto the disciples, Sit ye here, while I go and pray yonder. [37] And he took with him Peter and the two sons of Zebedee, and began to be sorrowful and very heavy.**
>
> **[John 18:15] And Simon Peter followed Jesus, and so did another disciple: that disciple was known unto the high priest, and went in with Jesus into the palace of the high priest.**

So here's a recap of what happened between those verses. Jesus hand-picked three of his guys to go to the Garden of Gethsemane instead of waiting with the others on the Mount of Olives. Judas shows up, somebody loses an ear, Jesus diffuses the tension, the three disciples bolt, Mark loses his clothing, and Jesus is taken to the secret trial. Outside, a small crowd gathers, knowing something is "going down." James must have gone up the hill to fetch/warn the others (since he vanishes from the narrative yet the women know to show up), but Peter and John gather their wits and follow Jesus to the place of the trial.

While this scene is normally fixated with Peter's betrayal, John's account reminds everybody how we even knew what happened in the trial—John was there. While Thomas is heading back to Galilee, Peter is ducking into an alley, and the others are scattering to the wind, John walks right up to the house of the high priest.

Bold!

This is odd for a variety of reasons. If the high priest knew John, then why did he let him witness the trial? Peter was questioned and bolted. With John, it was an open door. I've suspected it might have something to do with John the Baptist. If the high priest revered JB but hated JC, he might see JZ as an ally against this heretic (yuck, that was almost calculus). This would mean the high priest has not put the two together, which is possible since Jesus sent his disciples "out" during the major holidays. The apprentice of John the Baptist was to be respected. If they wanted to kill Jesus legally in the middle of the night, why would you want a witness who could talk smack about the unfairness of it all? Either they didn't notice John OR he was seen as being Team Caiaphas.

While John explains the obvious nature that the "staff" of the high priest must have known him to let him in, I'd like to speculate that if he was in fact a teenager, then he wouldn't be seen as a reliable witness for or against Jesus. If he was just a kid, then who cares if he's around?

# Exhibit D: At the Crucifixion

So who was the biggest villain? Caiaphas the High Priest? Herod the false king? Or Pontius Pilate the Roman? All of them had a reason to kill Jesus, and they all took part during that fateful evening, but when Jesus went up on the cross, it was under the authority of the Roman government.

Again, the plan was pretty sneaky. Nab Jesus during the middle of the night, put him on trial (both religious court and legal court), and get him nailed to the cross before anyone was the wiser. In your mental version, you picture a crowd shouting "Crucify him," right? Um...a crowd of Pharisees? Remember that the previous night the religious Jews stayed up past midnight for the Passover Ceremony, and everybody would have slept in the next day, which is why Jesus was taken at night and nailed to the cross before 9 AM in the morning (Roman time). The folks who were shouting "Hosanna" were probably waking up for late breakfast, gathered the family together, and began to head back into a very crowded Jerusalem. And what do they see outside the gates?

Jesus.

Nailed to a cross.

With a Roman crew standing guard.

What happened???

It does not say how many Romans were guarding the cross, but the previous night, Pilate sent a detachment of soldiers to arrest Jesus at the Mount of Olives. In case you didn't know, a detachment was somewhere between 100-1000 soldiers (depending on your source and time). If we just take a number in the middle (300), that is way too much just to arrest a single man.

Remember, they didn't plan to find Jesus at the Garden of Gethsemane—Jesus foiled their plans by turning himself in—they planned to get EVERYBODY sleeping on the Mount of Olives.

Because of this, the disciples BOLTED, with Thomas hightailing it all the way back to Galilee. Everybody else hid. Remember, though, that John gained access and was present at the foot of the cross. Eventually, the Galilean women like Mother Mary, Mary Magdalene, and others also were at the cross.

What were the orders given to the Romans?

A.  Obviously guard Jesus until he was dead. Nobody was to try to rescue him. As a result, you'd have to expect a few standing at the foot of the cross, and others would be positioned at the road, telling the shocked crowd to move along.

B.  Spies. Joining the Pharisees, they probably want to make arrests. Granted, they cut the head off the snake, but if they can arrest guys like Peter, Christianity would never get started. That's why they came with a detachment to arrest Jesus. They wanted to kill EVERYBODY.

Yet, John plops down at the foot of the cross and mourns and ministers to Jesus just like everyone else. This is in public, not some back door of Caiaphas's house. There is imminent danger of being arrested and put onto a fourth cross, yet no one thinks to do a thing with John. Again, I feel if he were just a kid of 15, he would have not been seen as either a threat or a disciple.

Remember, the scene ends for John when Jesus all but dismisses him by connecting Mother Mary and John as teacher and pupil.

**[John 19:26] When Jesus therefore saw his mother, and the disciple standing by, whom he loved, he saith unto his mother,**

**Woman, behold thy son! [27] Then saith he to the disciple, Behold thy mother! And from that hour that disciple took her unto his own home.**

That hour, John took her away. The raw emotions from his mother and Little Buddy must've been hard for him to endure, especially if John was a kid experiencing an execution for the first time.

## Exhibit E: Robin to Batman

So one of the last acts by Jesus is to let his mother know that he'd like her to take John under her wing, and conversely, John needs to learn from Mary.

Remember, this is the same kid whose mom (Zebedee's wife) comes with.

How is he mentioned? The Brother of James. The little brother.

Once we get to the Book of Acts, we see the disciples break up to begin evangelizing the world. According to tradition, Andrew died in Tracia, Phillip died in Turkey, Bartholomew, Thomas, and Matthew died in India, James Alphaeus died in Egypt, Judas Son of James died in Mesopotamia, and Simon died in Ethiopia. The disciples turned into international travelers (and martyrs). But as soon as we get to Acts 3, we see John as the sidekick to Peter. When they speak in tongues, their reaction is curious.

**[Acts 2:7] And they were all amazed and marveled, saying one to another, Behold, are not all these which speak Galileans?**

The reason I say the reaction is curious is that a grown, adult man has the capacity to be multilingual. Nothing alarming about that (I could force some Spanish). But what would be amazing? A 15 year old kid who knows a dozen languages. How is that possible given his youth?

By Acts 12, James is beheaded, Peter is doing his own thing, and Paul is stealing the spotlight. John? Crickets.

Again, I believe much of this has to do with his age. If he can't preach in Jewish synagogues until he reaches 30 (like Jesus), then it's no wonder he is silent during this era. Plus, he's supposed to be hanging out with Mary, so I suppose he's in graduate school. He simply does not have any stand up moments...yet.

## Exhibit F: His age at Patmos

The last argument for a young John is his activities leading to his arrest and imprisonment on Patmos. While I'll save most of the details for later, most scholars place the imprisonment around 95 AD. If John was grown and the same age as Jesus, he'd be over ninety, which is still possible, but becoming unlikely. If John was only 15 during the Gospels, and you tack on another sixty years, then he is still a robust 75 on his way to Patmos.

# CHAPTER THREE

# A PROMISE

Jump into that DMC DeLorean with me and rev it up to 88 mph...we're going back—to Genesis. We're not sure how long Adam served as a gardener before he got lonely and asked God for a partner, nor do we know how long God made Adam wait before...rib, poof, WOMAN! We're also not exactly sure how much time passed between Eve arriving in the Garden and...hiss, crunch, NAKED! However, from the moment Adam took a bite, he went from being super-Adam to mortal-Adam, and despite being shaped in perfection, his internal clock began to tick (slowly) to his eventual death. It's at the moment his internal clock began to tick down that God made an interesting promise. Genesis 3 describes a resetting of creation, right down to specific changes to Satan, Eve, and Adam. Along with the talk of tilling, childbirth, and slithering, God mentioned:

> **[Genesis 3:15] And I will put enmity between you and the woman, and between your seed and her seed.**
> **He will crush your head,**
> **and you will strike his heel.**

Okay, so it's not OBVIOUS that it is a promise of the Christ, but most scholars interpret this as a conflict between Christ and Satan. Overlay Revelation 12 with this moment, and it explains the purpose of Christ—to fix a broken world. Between the Garden and Bethlehem, God made a whole bunch of other promises, including the good ones (Abraham/father of nations) and the bad ones (Solomon/lose a nation). Dozens and dozens of promises were made and then fulfilled (a few books of the Bible) later.

The promise is not always fulfilled the way you expect it to be fulfilled.

Nor is it fulfilled on your timeline.

I want to go off on a tangent to discuss more promises, but this chapter has a specific subject and a specific promise. In the Preface, I promised to explain why I think John is one of the Two Witnesses, and to fulfill this promise, I need to dissect a minor promise made by Jesus.

## Mom! You didn't just...

The Gospel writers St. Matthew and St. Mark often get a bad rap for being so close in content, when in reality, they wrote their accounts at different times, places, and for different purposes.

So no plagiarism concerns.

Also, remember that while Matthew was one of the disciples, Mark was more likely than not just a kid during most of the Gospel era. His perspective came from Peter and others who proclaimed the message of Christ afterwards. After hearing these stories, he put together a "greatest hits" for the citizens of Rome, and possibly (later), the citizens of Alexandria, Egypt.

Matthew was there.

However, I'm not going to state one writer was right and the other was wrong. A police officer investigating a crime can interview two witnesses and get two separate accounts of the same event.

Perspective.

So let's set the scene.

According to my reckoning, Episode #180 of the Jesus Story happens during the days leading up to the final Passover. It is my belief that after hiding out for the winter months (following the death/murder/assassination & resurrection of Lazarus), Jesus and Company must go back to the Hornet's Nest (Jerusalem). Remember that the disciples KNEW going to Jerusalem meant a trap/death when they discussed going to save Lazarus. They warned Jesus about the obvious danger. "Literal" Thomas (I don't think he doubted; he was the only one who listened about Galilee) even said to Jesus **"Let us also go, that we may die with him"** (John 11:16).

After bringing Lazarus back to life and ruining the plans of the Pharisees to catch him, Jesus and Company know what a trip to Jerusalem means. Months earlier (Episode #147), while still in Galilee, Jesus talked about his impending death (Matt 17:22/Mark 9:30). So the tone of this trip should be a bit gloomy.

To reconcile the difference in the two accounts, picture Jesus in the middle of a dusty road. Matthew is walking on Jesus's left side, talking about prudent financial investments to help fund future ministry efforts. Up walks Mrs. Zebedee to his right side (Salome, Joanna, ??). She waits for Matthew to take a breath, then asks Jesus something. Stunned by the request, Matthew peels off, allowing Peter to step up to replace him at the left side WHILE James and John pull mom back, repeating the same request for themselves.

It's all about choreography.

There is no mistake made by Matthew or Mark.

Oh, the request?

Let's hear it first from Matthew:

**[Matthew 20:20] Then came to him the mother of Zebedee's children with her sons, worshipping him, and desiring a certain thing of him. [21] And he said unto her, What wilt thou? She saith unto him, Grant that these my two sons may sit, the one on thy right hand, and the other on the left, in thy kingdom. [22] But Jesus answered and said, Ye know not what ye ask. Are ye able to drink of the cup that I shall drink of, and to be baptized with the baptism that I am baptized with? They say unto him, We are able. [23] And he saith unto them, Ye shall drink indeed of my cup, and be baptized with the baptism that I am baptized with: but to sit on my right hand, and on my left, is not mine to give, but it shall be given to them for whom it is prepared of my Father.**

**[24] And when the ten heard it, they were moved with indignation against the two brethren. [25] But Jesus called them unto him, and said, Ye know that the princes of the Gentiles exercise dominion over them, and they that are great exercise authority upon them. [26] But it shall not be so among you: but whosoever will be great among you, let him be your minister; [27] And whosoever will be chief among you, let him be your servant: [28] Even as the Son of man came not to be**

**ministered unto, but to minister, and to give his life a ransom for many.**

Time to unpack.

Let's start with the ending. The disciples were indignant, which supports my choreography of having Matthew peel off. Who better than one of the "indignant" to write that they felt "indignant." A Holy-Spirit inspired Matthew would later understand the error of his narrow view.

Jesus chews them out by getting morbid. He brings up the Gentiles/Romans. Why? He explains that the Romans have a part to play but it is all God's plan. God>Romans>Disciples. This seems to suggest that the Gentiles will kill them (martyrs) because it's part of God's plan.

Then Jesus does something very subtle. If you were to visually sort the disciples from youngest to oldest (wait, we have no birth dates, do we)...well, which disciples still have MOMMY tugging on Jesus's sleeve? The lil' guys: John and James. Jesus puts the old guys (Matthew/Peter?) in their place by saying the little guy will get a big role and the big guy will be a servant. IE...get ready for new leadership when I'm gone.

Back up even further, and you'll realize that MOM specifically brought up her two boys for leadership roles. Strangely, Jesus did not shoot Mrs. Zebedee down but instead deferred to God by saying it was HIM that would decide such things in Heaven.

But on earth?

Ah...Jesus was a bit slippery in how he answered.

# A Metaphoric Baptism

Before we get to the heart of the matter, let's just compare the two accounts and see what Mark (via Peter) wrote about the same event (Episode #180).

**[Mark 10:35] And James and John, the sons of Zebedee, come unto him, saying, Master, we would that thou shouldest do for us whatsoever we shall desire. 36 And he said unto them, What would ye that I should do for you? [37] They said unto him, Grant unto us that we may sit, one on thy right hand, and the other on thy left hand, in thy glory. [38] But Jesus said unto them, Ye know not what ye ask: can ye drink of the cup that I drink of? and be baptized with the baptism that I am baptized with? [39] And they said unto him, We can. And Jesus said unto them, Ye shall indeed drink of the cup that I drink of; and with the baptism that I am baptized withal shall ye be baptized: [40] But to sit on my right hand and on my left hand is not mine to give; but it shall be given to them for whom it is prepared.**

**[41] And when the ten heard it, they began to be much displeased with James and John. [42] But Jesus called them to him, and saith unto them, Ye know that they which are accounted to rule over the Gentiles exercise lordship over them; and their great ones exercise authority upon them. [43] But so shall it not be among you: but whosoever will be great among you, shall be your minister: [44] And whosoever of you will be the chiefest, shall be servant of all. [45] For even the**

**Son of man came not to be ministered unto, but to minister, and to give his life a ransom for many.**

So except for the omission of Mrs. Zebedee, these two paragraphs are pretty much the same. The question is asked, Jesus clarifies, they agree to the clarification, Jesus clarifies Heaven, the disciples get rankled, Jesus tells them to expect things to be flipped, and another foreshadowing about death.

James and John shot BIG! The left and right hand in Heaven. But this also shows they are good listeners. They understood that Jesus would soon be killed. They heard him talk about it back in Galilee, and again with Lazarus, and now, heading to certain death, they accept the truth and even believe they might be killed soon also.

Their request is deferred, but Jesus first pulls apart their request. When he says **"Ye know not what ye ask."** he rolls his omniscient eyes when thinking of the horrors waiting for him with the crucifixion. These young punks want to die? They don't understand what's in store for Jesus. Wait...Jesus pauses. Peter will deny me, but these boys? These boys seem to be willing to die with me, just like Thomas.

So Jesus checks.

In typical Jesus fashion, he dumbs things down with figurative language. He wants to make sure the Zebedee brothers understand what they are saying. **"Can ye drink of the cup that I drink of? and be baptized with the baptism that I am baptized with?"** Christ's question does not literally speak of baptism. Remember, he's already been baptized in the Jordan River, so...figurative. Oh yeah, and who saw him get baptized?

John, John, and Andrew. My bet is both Zebedee brothers have already had the classic baptism. So...let's assume baptism=martyrdom.

Jesus understands they are both willing to die for their beliefs, which sets them apart from a disciple like Peter or the others who hid in the upper room (while Thomas was on his way to Galilee, mind you). Jesus changes the subject from talk about the afterlife to how they are willing to get there. He uses the metaphor of baptism because you pour water over the body. If there is no water, then...yup, a baptism of blood. This is not old age, a heart attack, or an accident Christ is speaking about—he's talking about a violent death.

Are you willing to be a martyr?

Instead of slinking off to find mom, the boys answer boldly.

**We can.**

Be careful what you wish for, boys.

## Jesus gets a 93.75%

So that was awkward.

Right in front of the other disciples, John and James let Christ know that they were able and willing to follow him through a torture, a public execution, and a restoration in Heaven (just no guaranteed seating). A short time later, Mary Magdalene is cleaning the lamb, John is chosen to find a donkey, and Easter Week is underway.

The four Gospels and the rest of the New Testament are so focused on the Christ story that there is not a lot of discussion about what happens to the disciples. There is good reason for that. Most of them died after the books of the NT were written.

We all know Peter and Paul died in Rome, but can you find it written down? Nope. Andrew? The good Judas? Matthew?

None of them get a mention because their deaths happened after the ink had dried (except for Revelation and the Gospel of John...we'll talk about that later).

Oh, wait.

We do have one (and I'm not talking about Judas Iscariot).

James.

Not James, son of Alphaeus (he was crucified in Egypt). Nor James the Just (thrown from temple/clubbed).

**[Act 12:1]About that time, King Herod reached out to harm some who belonged to the church. 2 He had James, the brother of John, put to death with the sword.**

While Judas Iscariot hung himself, and Stephen was stoned to death, James is the FIRST of the 12 disciples to get martyred.

As promised.

And he wasn't even the BELOVED DISCIPLE.

According to "tradition," here is what happened to the twelve disciples:

| | |
|---|---|
| Judas Iscariot | Hung himself |
| James, son of Zebedee | Beheaded |
| Simon Peter | Inverted crucifixion |
| Paul | Beheaded in Rome |
| Andrew | Crucified on Olive Tree |
| Philip | Crucified upside down |
| Bartholomew | Crucified/Flayed |
| Thomas | Speared to death |
| James, son of Alphaeus | Crucified by pagans |
| Matthew Levi | Burned in Ethiopia |

| | |
|---|---|
| Thaddeus/Judas | Arrows |
| Simon the Zealot | Sawed in half |
| Luke | Hanged in Olive Tree |
| Matthias | Stoned in Jerusalem |
| Barnabas | Stoned in Egypt |
| John | Old Age |

'Scuse me?

Old age?

The guy who cut in line so he could ask to be a martyr gets...old age. As you'll learn later in this series, I was so upset by this strange paradox that I stood over the "purported" tomb of St. John in Ephesus just to ask my question there. While I do like the idea of 1 of those 16 fellows getting to live happily ever after, it seems a bit off. So when I chased down the most reliable sources of the death, the guy who wrote that John "sleeps in Ephesus" as in, you know, he's dead in Ephesus, was also ex-communicated for being a heretic. He was called out for being a fraud, but his letter sent to Rome was kept as a fact. There is even confusion about his tomb since his body was not found. I'll get to this strange stuff later.

My point?

Jesus doesn't break his promises.

Having Christ operating at a 93% average is not a very awe-some God. He's not getting to Harvard with grades like that, is he? 93%. Wait...Christ didn't promise ALL his disciples that they could join in his bloody baptism metaphor. The only two he promised martyrdom to were James (1st beheaded) and John (died of old age).

What gives?

The same question must have gone through John's own mind a time or two, and by the time he wrote the Book of Revelation, the Epistles, and the Gospel of John, things were cleared up a little bit, which is why he ended his Gospel with another promise from Christ.

Which also has yet to be fulfilled.

To be continued, I guess.

# CHAPTER FOUR

# BOOT CAMP

So we're going to quickly flip through the Gospel of John to just review how John's account is a bit different. I'm not going to diminish it, trust me, but it is very different than the others. When the flipping ends, we're going to be with Jesus and John on the Mount of Olives.

Buckle Up.

Event 1: John gives a holistic view of Christ from Creation to the Jordan River, where he enters the story as an apprentice/disciple of John the Baptist. He witnesses the baptism first hand. Oh yeah, and we meet other disciples like Andrew, Peter, Philip, and Nathanael (??). Off we go to Galilee

Event 2: Christ/Bride metaphor is established at the wedding of Cana. Jesus leaves his Galilee disciples behind to…

(John reads Matthew, Mark, Luke's account of the temptation, skips to…)

Event 3: Arrive from the wilderness at Jerusalem just in time for the Passover, where he trashes the tables, meets Nicodemus, gathers up Judean disciples, nods goodbye to John the Baptist, and heads up to Galilee.

Event 4: Noting that MML did not write about it, John gives his account of stopping at Samaria on his way from Jerusalem and to Galilee. Here, we get the preview of ministering to Gentiles, as well as John specifically mentioning day and season (4 months to harvest=it's late spring).

Event 5: Noting that MML did not write about it, John writes about healing a nobleman's son when he returned to Galilee.

(John reads M&M's account of returning to the Sea of Galilee, which is an account about the first disciples waiting for Jesus to return. With both crews of disciples accounted for, John chooses to skip all the other details and jump into the public ministries that begin in the autumn (Feast of Tabernacles).

STOP THE FLIPPING! (for this chapter, anyway)

So this is an introduction into the mind of John for a moment. He is the glue that fills in the missing pieces of the puzzle. There is a very good reason his Gospel is 4th, and it's not because it's 4th place (I'll get to that in another chapter).

I stopped flipping because there is an entire summer missing from record. Again, John methodically explained things down to the day following Passover, referenced that harvest was in four months, added a couple small details, and then in Chapter 5 specifically sets the rest of the events, including MML's anecdotes, AFTER the Feast of Tabernacles.

So what happened during that summer?

It's hard to imagine, but....nothing happened?

Imagine having three months to spend with Christ during a summer, and afterwards, having nothing to write about.

NOTHING!?

Just ponder this gap for a few moments.

With MML, it's hard to see the gap even exists, but with John's very specific timekeeping (he was there, he knows), he leaves us with a calendar of events.

This also leaves us with a HUGE gap of three months or so.

What had just happened again? Jesus gathered up disciples, didn't he? First, he found his Galilean crew (John, James, Andrew, Peter, Philip, and Nathanael) who waited for his return by the lake. Then, after dealing with Satan, he returned to Jerusalem, where he picks up some other disciples (Thomas, Judas Iscariot, James Alphaeus, Judas of James, Simon the Zealot, Thaddeus?). When Jesus returns to Galilee for the classic "lake shore" moment of casting nets, he's already met the guys in the boat and now has the FULL crew.

And then to do nothing?

My explanation leads back to the title of this chapter...boot camp. Think about it...these guys have been called from all walks of life but none of them are scholars. Yes, they get the Holy Spirit AFTER the crucifixion, but most of them are a little ill equipped, aren't they?

Does Jesus want these guys out in the public without training?

I like to picture these guys leaving the shores of Galilee to then find some remote hillside, valley, ravine, where Christ can sit on the rock and just "talk" with his crew. Who says the crew is 100% men? We know Christ will pick his 12 after his ministry goes public, so this "summer crowd" is much larger. It has not been sifted yet (remember the drinking blood incident).

So John, along with all the others, spends three months or so alone with Christ, where they can ask any question and he can explain any mystery of life. What would you ask? Perhaps a question about the Platypus? Or mosquitos? Ask away, we have ninety days of doing nothing.

My theory supports a very young John, so it is possible an entire camp of followers, including Mrs. Z, could be nearby. Ultimately, Christ is looking for those who can be the spiritual torchbearers for Christianity when he leaves. Jesus is annoyed by crowds because they get in the way of preparing his mini-me's. He did not want to do it himself; he wanted humans to bring salvation to other humans (take that, Satan).

## My Elementary Teacher: Mr. Baptist

But for John, this is his second training section. Even though he is the youngest one, he's already been working with John the Elijah (err...Baptist), who has no peer among regular humans (just ask Jesus). John and Andrew weren't sent to some regular dude for religious training, they were sent to THE BEST.

Keep in mind, MML all wrote about the baptism, and instead of skipping it like he often does when MML cover an event, John amplified it, which should give us insight into the nuanced differences:

> **[John 1:29] The next day John saw Jesus coming toward him and said, "Look, the Lamb of God, who takes away the sin of the world! [30] This is He of whom I said, 'A man who comes after me has surpassed me because He was before me.' 31 I**

myself did not know Him, but the reason I came baptizing with water was that He might be revealed to Israel."

[32] Then John testified, "I saw the Spirit descending from heaven like a dove and resting on Him. [33] I myself did not know Him, but the One who sent me to baptize with water told me, 'The man on whom you see the Spirit descend and rest is He who will baptize with the Holy Spirit.' [34] I have seen and testified that this is the Son of God."

[35] The next day John was there again with two of his disciples. [36] When he saw Jesus walking by, he said, "Look, the Lamb of God!" [37] And when the two disciples heard him say this, they followed Jesus.

[38] Jesus turned and saw them following. "What do you want?" He asked.

They said to Him, "Rabbi" (which means Teacher), "where are You staying?"

[39] "Come and see," He replied. So they went and saw where He was staying, and spent that day with Him. It was about the tenth hour.

Yes, it never explicitly says John and Andrew here, but they are the two disciples that leave with him. John has others that will join Jesus later, but it is unclear who they are. There are some really cool things that can be inferred besides the two disciples.

Lamb of God!!!

Years before Mary Magdalene washes the feet of the paschal lamb, John the Baptist already knows Jesus is going to get killed. If he knows this well, so do John and Andrew, which is why he uses the phrase when pointing to Jesus. It seems that John the Elijah came back down to earth knowing the plan but he did not know what the Christ would look like (this is why I feel John the

Baptist did not come back from abroad until he reached 30). He's been training Andrew and John for the Christ, not for himself. All of the abstract concepts have already been told to these two, including the End Game. The two star students were handed off while the other crew waited for a few more months, when Jesus picked them up also.

## My Middle School Teacher: Mr. Christ

Next, John is recruited by the Son of God, where he spends three months in relative isolation before beginning a whirlwind ministry, which will leave him with the moniker "The Beloved Disciple" by the time he ends.

While the ministry of Christ is for "All of us" obviously, one very practical purpose of it was to train these pillars of the future church to spread the fire of Christianity. And like most teachers, Christ waited for the cream to rise to the top. By the time we get to Passover Week, we know who the A students were (they all have special gifts. Not everybody is meant for college, I know): John, Peter, James, and sometimes, Andrew.

(We'll get back to the rest of the Gospel next chapter)

These four get the special training of the transfiguration, find the donkey, set up the Passover meal, listen to the End Times talk, and even go down to the Garden of Gethsemane with him. John gets to be at the cross. In my theory, John was 1 of the 2 disciples on the road to Emmaus, who got trained virtually by a resurrected Christ in disguise (when else did Peter "Son of a beloved father" see the Lord?).

I'm rushing through the Mr. Christ years because hanging with Jesus seems like it would lend itself to obvious lessons. After all, John finishes his own gospel with these words:

> **[John 21:25] And there are also many other things which Jesus did, the which, if they should be written every one, I suppose that even the world itself could not contain the books that should be written. Amen.**

Okay, John, we get it…you had a good teacher.

## Guest Speakers: Moses and Elijah

MML all describe the transfiguration, even though the guy who spent several days on the mountain did not add a word. Come on, John. In fact, it almost seemed like a secret between Christ and his star students. Listen to how Mark put it:

> **[Mark 9:9] And as they came down from the mountain, he charged them that they should tell no man what things they had seen, till the Son of man were risen from the dead. [10] And they kept that saying with themselves, questioning one with another what the rising from the dead should mean. [11] And they asked him, saying, Why say the scribes that Elias must first come? [12] And he answered and told them, Elias verily cometh first, and restoreth all things; and how it is written of the Son of man, that he must suffer many things, and be set at nought. [13] But I say unto you, That Elias is indeed come, and they have done unto him whatsoever they listed, as it is written of him.**

Okay, so Jesus thought so much of them that he spilled the beans with the old "John=Elijah" mind-melter. Most Christians struggle to wrap their brains around this one, and we have the

Holy Spirit. However, I want you to notice that verse nine has Christ telling them not to spill any of the beans until after the resurrection

Jesus was much better at making metaphors, but let me try...

This "transfiguration" scene is like a teacher inviting two guest speakers to class. For a Phy Ed teacher, it would be like introducing your friend, the Olympian. For an English teacher, it would be like having J.R.R. Tolkien show up in your Google Meet. Ups your cred with the kids, right. For Jesus, he just summons two dead guys from the depths of Sheol. Beelzebub is down in the underworld taking attendance (Ben Stein voice): "Moses? Moses? Moses? Son of Amram? Aaron, where is your brother?"

I guess if you're the Christ, you can summon anybody you want.

But wow, what guest speakers!!!!

Think about the stuff Moses could talk about.

And Elijah...he was taken alive into Heaven, only to...

"Hey Jesus, why did we just see a very dead Elijah?"

"Mark 9:12-13"

"Okay, thanks Jesus."

Jesus was a tough teacher who made his students figure things out. Clearly, John impressed Jesus, which is why this wasn't his last boot camp.

## My High School Teacher: Ms. Mary

As Jesus was dying on the cross, ending his earthly ministry, the story of John was just beginning, even if it felt like the end. Unlike the other disciples, John is allowed to be with Jesus in his dying moments. He'd been with him during the final evening for the Last Supper, and even later in the night, at the Garden of Gethsemane. When Jesus was arrested (James took off), he quickly found Jesus at the shared housing complex (my theory) of Annas and Caiaphas, the high priests (and then Peter took off). When Jesus was taken to Pilate, then Herod, and back to Pilate, someone had to witness this. While Mary Magdalene shows up for the Easter story, I think the best witness for these early morning events remains John.

When Jesus is brought out to be scourged, and then later, nailed to the cross, I think John might be the one who remains the whole time. Yes, Peter and James probably saved the crowd of Christians from impending doom (Satan/Judas showed up with a whole lot of soldiers meant to arrest/kill Christians at the base of the Mount of Olives); however, only the women were brave enough to stick their necks out at Golgotha (Thomas was already heading to Galilee :).

And John?

As the hours tick by, John is joined by the Virgin Mary, Mary Magdalene, and others as Jesus quickly fades because of the scourging. In fact, he only spends about three hours hanging in torment before he does something very peculiar.

**[John 19:26] When Jesus therefore saw his mother, and the disciple standing by, whom he loved, he saith unto his mother, Woman, behold thy son! [27] Then saith he to the disciple, Behold thy mother! And from that hour that disciple took her unto his own home.**

Remember, John is the Beloved Disciple, and this account is something that MML do not bring up. Apparently, MML must interview Mary Magdalene because look at what it says. "That hour" John took the Virgin Mary to his own home (ruining some wonderful paintings showing Mary holding Jesus, huh). Even if the "leaving" isn't literal or immediate, there are other things to ponder about what Jesus said to them.

Remember, Mrs. Zebedee is still very much alive. John doesn't need a mother.

Remember, the Virgin Mary has other "sons and daughters" to take care of her after this (James, Joses, Simon, Jude, and the daughters) Yes, they might be nieces and nephews, but they are legally bound to each other.

Remember, there is a small chance Joseph is still alive and working in the carpentry shop (Isn't this the Carpenter's son=could be around still).

Remember, John goes on missions during the Book of Acts with Peter.

This is not a joint welfare program for John and Mary.

This is the world's best student being teamed up with the world's greatest teacher.

My philosophy on the Son of God being born in a manger is that the Trinity was trying to prove something to Satan about the capacity of humanity. Satan said we were worthless; billions of humans had proven him right by sinning. Jesus was born into vulnerable flesh, surrounded by sin, yet after thirty years of living with it around him, he still hadn't sinned...then he got baptized and forgiven for sins he didn't commit.

"This is my Son, of whom I am well-pleased"

THEN...the Holy Spirit descended upon Jesus, making him in my mind "Super-Jesus." The Son of God had the human veil lifted and he walked and spoke with ultimate authority from that moment on. The first test was over...time to get the Church ready.

Mary taught Jesus. Mary raised Jesus. Ask yourself if your two-year-old Jesus is omniscient and omnipotent. If yes, that makes language and potty-training quite unnecessary, doesn't it? He's got it figured out if completely omniscient and omnipotent at birth. He can make the rattle float from the floor and up to the crib because...omnipotent. If two, then why not earlier. If not two, when...four, five, twelve, sixteen, twenty-three...

See, I love the idea of Jesus being a regular dude because that proves Satan wrong. What does it prove to have him built to be perfect and then not sin? I think Mary and Joseph, devoting 24-7-365 to the child that is the Son of God, helped create the perfect child. Yes, he was the Son of God also, but I think they gave him all of the tools and understanding to resist humans. Read Psalm 91 and it does appear as if a "hedge" was place around Jesus, keeping supernatural efforts from Satan to tempt him (remember, Job came close). However, Jesus was surrounded by evil on all sides, but Mary and Joseph's training (remember, he knew the basics before he went to the Pharisees at the age of 12) helped keep him grounded and strong. Mary was the greatest Sunday School Teacher EVER!

Now, Jesus looks down from the cross and connects his pupil with his former teacher.

History teaches that John brought Mary from the Holy Lands to modern day Turkey, where he built a house for her on a hill overlooking Ephesus. John almost fades from Biblical history as he tends to Mary. How did they spend these decades? I'd like to believe she taught all those things she pondered in her heart.

And when the Romans knocked on John's door, his training was complete.

He was now ready to graduate to Revelations.

# CHAPTER FIVE

# A PROPHECY UNPACKED

We left off at the Silent Summer, as we were flipping through the Gospel of John. After John sets a firm date AFTER the Feast of Tabernacles (harvest=fall), he steps back to let the narratives of Matthew, Mark, and Luke (MML) be told as they recorded and witnessed them. John skips over almost six months of classics like the Galilee storms, demons, crowd issues, selecting Matthew, and final correspondence with John the Baptist.

He briefly records anecdotes like meeting Mary Magdalene, talks of a House Divided, Blasphemy against the Holy Spirit, and a whole bunch of parables happened in the spring (with a Passover reference) before rejoining MML with the loaves and fishes anecdote.

After this, John breaks into a long, isolated anecdote about Christ challenging the crowds, throwing some harsh challenges their way (John 7&8), and watching as he loses his crowd and even some of his disciples he trained during the Silent Summer.

John concludes by finishing what Jesus did during his second recorded Passover (Chapters 9&10).

Flip: Spring and summer in Galilee, more miracles, etc.

Flip: Transfiguration

Flip: Touring through western Judea

Flip: A bunch of Luke's parables

Ah! John finally stops to write when he realizes MML skipped a trip to Jerusalem during the Feast of Dedication (winter). Once again, he gives an independent account of Christ's trip for this required Jewish festival, including what happened right after they left: Lazarus dying. Thanks to John, we know this event happened three months before his death at Passover, and established a conspiracy of Pharisees to kill Christ (was Lazarus poisoned to draw him back?). John describes how Jesus purposely waits for three days after Lazarus dies, which is when the Pharisees left, and THEN Jesus went into the defused death trap. Cool story, John.

John concludes chapter eleven by summarizing that they hid out for the next three months since their lives were on the line due to the conspiring. He bridges these three months by saying they came out of hiding to head to the Passover.

Flip: Jericho (who's that in the tree?)

Flip: The time mom brought up being a martyr (so embarrassing).

BAM! John puts MML in their places by specifically stating when Mary (Magdalene) washed his feet. Matthew and Mark didn't make any date claims, but they left it out of place in the wrong context. So John specifies that the event happened **"six days before the Passover"** (12:1). Why? To our star student, he understood the symbolism of the Passover, including that the sacrificial lamb was brought into the house for spoiling before it was sacrificed. Before bringing the lamb into the house (Nisan 10), the lamb had to be cleaned (Nisan 9th), which is five days before the lamb is killed (Nisan 14) and SIX days before the celebration of the Passover (freedom day). John gets why it matters.

Flip: All the Easter stuff that happened on Nisan 11th

Flip: All the Easter stuff that happened on Nisan 12th

Flip: All the Easter stuff that happened on Nisan 13th

Flip: All the End Times talk Jesus said on the Mount of Olives.

Hold on, what?

Isn't it wild that John skips over something he was specifically a part of? Now, remember that MML record it in a wild arrangement of details, which John usually can't tolerate. So in a way, he's cool with the way they wrote it. Another thing to think about is...John has the FULL account already written. Remember, the books of the Bible were not written as an installment series (stay tuned to see what happens to Jesus next...). No, the Gospel of John was written AFTER he wrote the Book of Revelation (we'll get back to that later). He knows his account is out there, so he skips it in his own Gospel. Funny.

But there are some key details to notice that I'd like to draw your attention to. For a moment, forget all the doom and destruction and look at the context of the scene. Mark records that:

**[Mark 13:3] And as he sat upon the mount of Olives over against the temple, Peter and James and John and Andrew asked him privately, [4 ]Tell us, when shall these things be? and what shall be the sign when all these things shall be fulfilled?**

Even though it is subtle, notice how this is an audience of four: Andrew, Peter, James, and John. Is everyone asleep? Did Jesus step away? How private was private? Given the context and subject, I think it is reasonable to assume the conversation is meant for his star-students.

As much as I want to jump into each of the things Jesus says and compare it to what John wrote down in his account, I'm going to stay focused on a few stray hairs.

## Two More Promises

Imagine being those four when Jesus starts referencing the Antichrist, global catastrophe, and the end of Christianity (which they are just beginning). How traumatic! Especially if you are a kid. Granted, being Master of the Universe and Creator of All Things might desensitize you to the little things (did I just step on an ant?), but John is tender and young.

Gulp!

Out of nowhere, Jesus seems to pivot from dreadful talk of the future (Hey, you asked for details) to a peculiar promise and reassurance to the kid who's freaked out: Mark 13:10 **"And the gospel must first be published among all nations."**

First...

Before any of these things happen...

ALL...nations...

This would get me to calm down if I were John. Think about it. When Jesus said this, Christianity was limited to a small hill in Judea and in a few Magi homes somewhere out there in the wilderness. Heck, we're not even sure what's out past Atlantis, right? All nations? We can't get Samaria to behave! With modern lenses, we know that Christians didn't get to North America for 15 centuries, and even after that, there were isolated nations in various jungles that didn't see us until when...1900s? John knew it was a big world, far bigger than any man could travel in a lifetime, right? So...heart calms...what else, Jesus?

After Jesus seems to summarize the Horses/Seals 1-5, he suddenly fixates on the events of Seal Six. Remember, the original question that (John) asked Jesus was "WHEN" the End Times was happening. Jesus knows it is a complicated answer involving breaking of seals, which are dependent on factors, lots of details, details that God knows, and red-tape, and yadda, yadda, yadda… "but when the Sixth Seal is broken, I can tell you how many days you have left? How's that for an answer?"

For a scholar like John, who knows prophecy thanks to his teachers, talk of the End of the World didn't begin with Jesus. But when Jesus transitions to the Sixth Seal talk and then connects it to the Abomination of Desolation (Jesus using his Yoda voice: "A prophecy misread could have been")

Huh?

(no Yoda voice): The Abomination of Desolation is not HISTORY it is PROPHECY.

John: Ah, so the Daniel prophecy involving specifically one thousand—

Jesus: Yep, when the Sixth Seal is broken, you can count it down to the day.

John breathes a big sigh of relief. First, he was promised that the Sixth Seal stuff wouldn't begin until AFTER the Gospel was published/preached/spread to all nations. Now he also knows that the world won't end until the Daniel Stuff happens too.

In the back of his mind, though, he remembers another promise. Jesus promised him he'd be a martyr, didn't he? For James, that promise was kept just a few years after this moment on the Mount of Olives. For Peter, it happened a few decades later when he was crucified upside down in Rome. For John…OH THAT'S RIGHT! HISTORY SAID HE DIED OF OLD AGE!!!!!

Sensing John's questions (as well as Jason Willis's consternation on January 17th, 2021), Jesus leans forward, looks right at John, and says:

Mark 13:30: **"Verily, I say to you, that this generation shall not pass, till all these things be fulfilled."**

Peter: He's not looking at me when he said that. Oh no.

James: He promised me a martyr's death, so I'm not lasting to the End Times.

John: why is he looking right at me?

Matthew 24:34: **"Verily I say to you, THIS GENERATION shall not pass, till all these things be fulfilled."**

Collective: Hmm….Is he talking about the End Times generation or Us?

James: As soon as we begin preaching to nations, aren't we part of the generation that begins breaking seals?

Peter: Sweet! Maybe I'll see Jesus return before I have to die a terrible death.

John: No guys, he's really burning a hole right at me with his gaze.

Luke 21:32: **"Verily I say to you, THIS GENERATION will not pass away, till all be fulfilled."**

Peter: Why is he looking at John like that? I'm feeling jealous again…

James: Is he talking about the folks on the Mount of Olives? Could GENERATION mean everybody on the hill? Or all living humans? That would mean the End Times could happen within a century!

John: But I can't witness something that takes more than a thousand years? Either Jesus is mistaken or…he's not telling me something or….oh, wait…

## A Forgotten Promise

It is just conjecture that Jesus looked right at John, but if you visualize this scene with only four people, this seems to narrow the meaning. Scholars have contemplated this promise to mean quite a bit. Early evangelists rushed around the Middle East trying to get everyone right with Christ because they thought Jesus was coming back, you know, before THAT generation passed on. When historians recorded 100% death of all the folks alive when Jesus said it, the interpretation shifted THIS to mean the folks of the final End Times generation. Scholars have even defined "generation" to mean forty years. Now, I feel that interpretation is made in error. I believe that when Jesus promised John that the countdown wouldn't start until the Sixth Seal stuff and Daniel stuff, he wasn't talking about all the seals remaining uncracked. Nope, I think the first seal cracked when we began preaching to all nations. They've been cracking more frequently of late, but like John, I'm still waiting on the very obvious sixth seal.

Speaking of John waiting, what was my point?

I feel Jesus looked right into John's eyes and told him "you're going to be there at the end." My interpretation of that verse is that John will get his promised martyr's death on the most epic stage he could have imagined: surrounded by the Antichrist, his Prophet, the Whore of Babylon, and even Apollyon swirling around looking for a fight. You want a good death, kid?

Promises.

So yes, I reject John dying of old age. The rest of this book will defend my theory.

Yet even for John, hearing this theory for the first time, he must have been taken aback. He asked to be a martyr, and Jesus seems to counter it by saying he's going to wait...a long time!

Yet there is another thought that might creep into his mind.

This isn't the first time Jesus said something like this.

Months earlier, before Easter, and before the martyr promise, Jesus is prepping his disciples for his death/resurrection plan when he dropped this line on THEM right before taking Peter, James, and John to the transfiguration:

**[Mark 9:1]: Verily I say unto you, That there be some of them that stand here, which shall not taste of death, till they have seen the kingdom of God come with power.**

This is echoed in:

**[Matt 16:28] Verily I say unto you, There be some standing here, which shall not taste of death, till they see the Son of man coming in his kingdom.**

Everybody but Jesus tastes death, right?

So who is Jesus talking about?

Remember, his crowd is composed of the disciples, so they=disciples.

Which one won't taste death?

And another thing...when does Jesus return...in his kingdom?

Yes, they all lived long enough (except for Judas) to see Jesus return from death, but that is not what he's talking about. Jesus is talking about the END OF THE STORY.

(Do you see a case building for John?)

# NECK DEEP

We'll come back to the Gospel of John in a later chapter, and we'll definitely return to some of those promises that Jesus made to John, but for now, we're going to leave the familiar texts found in the Bible and go to a source that will cause anxiety and nausea for most students—research papers.

What are we researching?

While the four Gospels do a fine job summarizing the three years of Christ's active ministries, along with a few anecdotes about the rest of this life, the next book of the Bible, Acts, covers the next three decades in 24,000 words, which, if evenly distributed, is less than a thousand words per year. The opening chapters begin right after the Easter story but quickly start jumping years at a time, and by the time we get to Saul-Paul, the story goes off on a tangent and never returns to what happened to the other disciples. Nor does it even mention what happened to Paul.

What about the epistles?

Again, mostly Paul, but even they were about message and not context.

Our research is trying to understand what happened to John between the Easter Story and Patmos, but to find out the answers, we'll have to turn to historical records instead of the Bible. Oh yeah, and a big research paper also.

## **The History of the Church**

As I said, a big research paper! When teaching research, we discuss "source credibility" when selecting material to put into a research paper. I want to be honest that both names I'm about to mention have some issues of credibility, but it's far from a cop interviewing a drunk hobo who witnessed a crime from a dark alleyway. Around the year 300ish AD, Rome had a new emperor, Constantine the Great, who did something very different from his predecessors. First, he stopped killing Christians (about time). Then, he decided to tolerate Christians (how noble). Shorty after, he began to promote Christianity (seriously...is this a trick).

Times were a-changing.

History looks back at this sliver of time as the creation of the Roman Catholic Church, even though that happened centuries earlier. Yes, there was a Bishop of Rome, as well as bishops elsewhere around Christendom, but as a whole, they were an underground organization just trying not to be wiped out by the Romans. Not only did persecution abruptly end during the reign of Constantine, but he helped Christian leaders come out from the holes they'd been hiding in. After three centuries under rocks, Christian leaders stepped into the bright lights of Rome, but there was an issue—different churches had different traditions, and even variant texts.

Constantine the Great earned his moniker not because of his moral authority but because he was an efficient organizer. Looking upon the chaos of his new religion, he understood that something needed to be done, so he helped organize a little meeting later known as the Council of Nicaea. You know…the Nicene Creed! What was the purpose of church leaders coming up with a creed? So everyone could agree what it meant to be "Christian."

Dig into this time period, and you can easily twist the words and efforts of the church elders as they tried to find common ground and "orthodoxy" for this new Roman Catholic Church. Within a century, we'd also get Biblical canon so that we'd have a solid foundation on which to build. What a fascinating era to live, huh?

One of the leaders of this time period was the Bishop of Caesarea in Palestine (Rome had bulldozed Jerusalem centuries earlier). Bishop Eusebius (U See B.S.?) not only had an important voice (even when he was wrong on issues) but he also received an important commission…a history of the church.

Yep, the boss, Emperor Constantine, had a curiosity about the faith of his mother, St. Helena, and wanted to know what he was getting into. As a result, Bishop Eusebius wrote what would become a 434 page Penguin Classic translated by G.A. Williamson about all the things that happened from the time of Christ into the present.

How's that for pressure?

Did Constantine pick the right guy? Was it an infallible research paper? Having read it, you can certainly see that his heart was in the right place. Today, we have dozens of denominations with different colored lenses, which is why this important " shoe" does not fit all those different feet. Modern scholarship can be cruel to the legacy of both Emperor Constantine and Bishop Eusebius, but his historical record is the only surviving historical record of the era, so…

But have you read it?

Oh, boy, does it have some cool background!

But this is not a man who's trying to define Christianity according to his opinion. He made a big research paper, and looked up the works of writers with firsthand, or even second hand, knowledge of what the heck happened. It was the dark age of Christianity, after all.

## The Eusebius 'Notes" Version?

Quick recap of Christianity
- Barnabas has great success
- Thomas sends Thaddeus to Abgar
- Thaddeus tells Abgar of Jesus and how Jesus destroyed the gates of the Underworld
- Matthias elected to replace Judas
- Stephen becomes a leader
- James the Just rises to prominence
- Phillip encounters Simon the Magus
- Pilate conveys Christ's story to Tiberius
- Herods change/Pilate commits suicide
- 37-41 AD Gaius Caligula

- Famine strikes the entire world
- Claudius rules 41-54 AD
- James Zebedee killed by sword
- Herod struck dead by Angel
- Peter confronts Simon the Magus in Rome
- Gospel of Mark written for Romans
- Jews expelled from Rome, move to Asia Minor
- Paul Active in his ministries
- 30,000 Jews killed during Passover Riot (54 AD)

Okay, so that was the first two decades. Ask yourself this question: Where was John, the Beloved Disciple? I stopped the recap because we reach a name many are familiar with: Nero! Yes, Nero is the guy who had Peter and Paul killed, but I firmly disagree with the camp that feels that **THIS** is when John wrote Revelation as a figurative code for Christianity going to hell. I'll explain why in a bit.

But Nero was nasty, so let's keep our summary going:
- A "False" Christ attempted to siege Jerusalem.
- Paul's Trial Advances
- Luke writes his accounts
- Jews turn attention to James the Just
- Empress Agrippina ruled Nero's early years
- Nero eliminates public tortures
- In 59, Nero kills his mother
- Debauchery and art filled Nero's life while his empire grew
- In order to annex land for his new Golden House, Nero blames Christians on starting the fire.

- Nero has Peter and Paul killed as part of the lie (64 AD)
- Nero's power quickly fails and the senate condemns him
- He commits suicide in 68 AD

Following Nero, the next stage of Christianity is the Fall of Jerusalem. Remember, most of the known names from the Gospels are dead, leaving us with James the Just (the brother/cousin of Jesus) and John (where is he?).

Eusebius has wonderful details about what went down, but that's mostly due to the primary sourcing of Josephus. Here is a summary of the events around 70 AD:

- James the Just is universally regarded as the most righteous man around
- J the J is secretly the brother of Jesus and Jude
- J the J proclaims Christ at Passover
- J the J is thrown from the Temple and killed with a club when the fall didn't kill him.
- The city was mortified by what took place, which leads to...
- In 66 AD, Gallus failed to siege Jerusalem with 40,000 troops.
- Lost 6,000 on his retreat to Caesarea. Jews grew confident.
- Christians fled, seeing it as a sign.
- Nero sent Vespasian before his death
- Rome went through 3 leaders.
- Vespasian gave the army to his son, Titus.
- Titus prepared his 50,000 troops for a long siege.

- Titus waited until 3,000,000 Jews had gathered for the Passover.
- Titus attempts to give the Jews a chance to surrender
- And then levels the city.

Eusebius gathers up some pretty gnarly accounts of the destruction of Jerusalem, which is probably due to the fact that Jews often turned against Christians during the three centuries of Church history. After three centuries of shared persecution by the Romans, the Jews and Christians were not on good terms.

Seeing it as a sign, most Christians had already fled for Petra or for the churches started by Paul, including the seven churches in Turkey (Asia Minor).

## So Where was John?

Eusebius quotes and cites his way through the years after Christ, which is where many of our traditional knowledge comes from. He tells us that Peter was crucified, how Paul was executed, and several other important deaths. Lots of history. Lots. I wouldn't be forthright if I didn't say I had a disagreement with Eusebius when he writes the following summary:

**Book 3, Chapter 1: Thomas, tradition tells us, was chosen for Parthia, Andrew for Scythia, John for Asia, where he remained til his death at Ephesus.**

According to…? Tradition? Seriously, Eusebius. You can't claim facts without a citation. Now, I'll chase down this "John died at Ephesus" claim later, but for now, I'm going to jump to some other anecdotes about John that will add to your understanding of the Beloved Disciple. First, Eusebius confirms that John was a prisoner of Domitian while at Patmos until Nerva succeeded to the throne, which is a minor debate with modern scholars on the writing of the Book of Revelation. I'm with Eusebius.

OTHER SOURCES:

**Tertullian**, in his Apology, speaks of Domitian as having banished some Christians, and afterwards giving them leave to return home: probably intending St. John, and some others.

**Origen**, explaining something in Matthew, says: 'James, the brother of John, was killed with a sword by Herod. And a Roman emperor, as tradition teaches, banished John into the island Patmos for the testimony which he bore to the word of truth.

**Victorinus**, bishop of Pettaw about 290, again and again says that John was banished by Domitian, and in his reign saw the Revelation.

**Jerome**, in his Book of Illustrious Men, says: "Domitian in the fourteenth year of his reign raising the second persecution after Nero, John was banished into the island Patmos, where he wrote the Revelation."

**Sulpicius Severus** says, that 'John the apostle and evangelist, was banished by Domitian into the island Patmos where he had visions, and where he wrote the book of the Revelation.'

**Isidore**, of Seville, near the end of the sixth century, says, "Domitian raised a persecution against the Christians. In his time the apostle John having been banished into the island Patmos saw the Revelation."

I'm firmly in the Eusebius camp with this one. 95 AD, yup!

While confirming this detail, he writes 3:20: **At that time too the apostle John, after his exile on the island, re-**

**sumed his residence at Ephesus, as the early Christian tradition records.**

Okay, so not everything was written down for Eusebius to cite, but the tradition is that John lived in Ephesus prior to Patmos and also afterwards. One of the traditions has his bringing the Virgin Mary with him to Ephesus. Where do I get that?

Vacation. Yes, as I said earlier, I had so many questions about the life of John that I took a vacation with my wife to Rome, Patmos, and Ephesus. Prior to Paul's ministry, Ephesus was a hub for ancient paganism, where shrines of Artemis/Diana brought worshippers far and wide to modern day Turkey. I visited those ruins. They were impressive; I can't imagine how impressive they were back in the day. Paul saw it as a challenge, and went right down to those Dirty Diana Devotees and tossed the cleansing water of Christ in their faces. Whether Paul, or the other Christianized Jews knew it at the time, the Church needed to take root at places other than Israel, and by the time Titus came with his metaphoric bulldozers, Christian embers were beginning a blaze that would become the Seven Candlesticks in Revelation. Although tradition does not tell us WHEN he brought Mary, the latest date for the move would have been 70 AD, which means he lived there for at least a few decades. I like to picture him moving her earlier than that since we have little record of him in the Book of Acts after the first few years (and even then, he was sidekick to Peter). If Mary had younger children-cousins (a debate for another time), she might not have been able to do the move for a few years.

The original foundation of the house is still found in Ephesus. The rebuilt structure is on a wooded mountain slope, but built in a little "dip" in the hill, so that the structure isn't seen from the valley below. There is a natural spring providing water and the air is sweet. 2,000 years later, it's a place where I'd consider retiring. If it was John's secret base for preaching in Ephesus, it makes sense; however, if it is the place where master and apprentice trained, it's a perfect place to focus.

## Darth Domitian

Lurking in even darker shadows than a mountain cabin was a figure that came to the Roman throne in 81 AD—Emperor Domitian. I have a wild theory about the Seven Heads of the Beast (Antichrist) based on something that John later writes. In fact, I want to write a whole Bible study about it, but I'll save that for another day. First, let's look at what John did write:

> **[Revelation 17:7] And the angel said unto me, Wherefore didst thou marvel? I will tell thee the mystery of the woman, and of the beast that carrieth her, which hath the seven heads and ten horns.**
> **[8 ]The beast that thou sawest was, and is not; and shall ascend out of the bottomless pit, and go into perdition: and they that dwell on the earth shall wonder, whose names were not written in the book of life from the foundation of the world, when they behold the beast that was, and is not, and yet is. [9] And here is the mind which hath wisdom. The seven heads are seven mountains, on which the woman sitteth. [10] And there are seven kings: five are fallen, and one is, and the other is not yet come; and when he cometh, he must continue a short space. [11] And the beast that was, and is not, even he is the eighth, and is of the seven, and goeth into perdition. [12] And the ten horns which thou sawest are ten kings, which have**

**received no kingdom as yet; but receive power as kings one hour with the beast. [13] These have one mind, and shall give their power and strength unto the beast.**

What Biblical scholar or amateur hack hasn't taken a crack at these verses? But I'd like you to pay close attention to the most literal of the lines, verse 10.

According to the angel:

Heads=kings

Fallen=dead

Is=alive

Not yet come=the future.

Okay, so let's just recap a bit. John was shown a "Beast" with Seven Heads, and apparently, each dead head (not the Grateful Dead) has some sort of connection to the Antichrist. These dead heads were rulers, or kings, too. When John wrote this down, or specifically heard it from the angel, in 95 AD, five of the seven kings were already dead (Yes, I made a list of prime candidates) and one of them would appear in the future (Yes, I've got a Nazi-riffic candidate for that one, also) but the EASIEST ONE to figure out is the "is" (okay, that sounded strange). PRESENT TENSE RULER! Yes, I think it is the guy who arrested John because any other Roman Emperor (including Nero) pales in comparison. Why?

Not much is know about Domitian's early life, but his brother was the general who leveled Jerusalem. He was also a general, and loved the military so much that even after becoming Emperor, he wore his military uniform. He was violently homophobic and brought back horrifying penalties for crimes. He was a scary dude! He brought Rome to a dystopian government model of efficiency through terror and overhauled Rome's military to be at its peak efficiency. Oh, and he declared himself a deity (nothing out of the norm, there). Yet unlike his peers and predecessors, he did something unique. He privately brought back ancient Roman religions (forget those Greek God knock-offs), which included worshipping a four-faced version of Minerva.

Once versed in the dark lore, he turned his sights to Christianity. Taking up a dropped policy, he decided it was time to use the data from the old census to hunt down and exterminate any Jew with royal blood (bit late, but still wicked). His extermination was so complete that his bounty hunters brought him "a name" that was recognized—Jude.

Not Jude himself, but the bounty hunters still found two grandsons of Jude. To recap, they brought him the grandsons of a guy who may or may not have been a cousin of Christ. According to Eusebius, Domitian took one look at the calloused country-bumpkins and dismissed them (ironically allowing them to return to their successful ministries).

Maybe Domitian wasn't in the mood to witness torture and torment that day, but he was usually in the mood for blood. Roman historians wrote about his hidden and perverse cruelty, and that even socially, his dinner parties were so black and funereal that the guests would be paralyzed with fear.

Fun guy, huh?

He even had an epic death. According to some accounts, he was killed by a Christian assassin who seized an opportunity for revenge and to save Christendom. Ask yourself, if you could run-over the Antichrist (or Hitler) crossing the street, would you do it? Well, his assassin, a member of the household staff, took the chance, mortally wounding Domitian, who managed to kill his killer. Yes, he went out killing!

Seven Antichrist kings. One who is...Domitian.

## **The Execution of John**

Wait! I thought John died of old age in Ephesus. Isn't that what tradition says?

There is another tradition, cited only in reference, of a horrifying account of John and Domitian being brought together to the same place. According to the legend (cited by Tertullian), John was arrested.

Imagine being one of those bounty-hunter types looking for church leaders. When you stumble upon John, you're fishing for someone who'd make the Emperor happy. Once you get John talking, you suddenly realize that not only is he a Christian leader, but that he might be...wait for it...THE John. Yes, the guy from all the stories. Remember, the age issue (he's a spry 75) might make them question this truth, but if John opened his mouth, they would have known they caught the biggest fish in the seas.

So they bring him to Rome. Apparently, Domitian wanted the execution to be a big deal, so he chose to have it happen at the Coliseum in front of a big crowd. The "Latin Gate" is supposed to be the exact spot it happened. Again, this Urban Legend has a bunch of variations, including some where Domitian has him poisoned, but the most popular version has Domitian ordering a large vat of boiling oil.

I guess it makes sense...we don't want anybody coming back to life, do we? Boiling in oil would be horrific and when all is said and done, there wouldn't be anything but liquid goop to bury. That is an efficient execution!

So the cauldron was rolled in, the fires were lit, a platform was built, a crowd gathered, and Emperor Domitian showed up to see what all of the fuss was about. An agitated 75-year-old man is brought to the cauldron, walks up the stairs, and is tied to some sort of mechanism that would allow him to be lowered into the cauldron.

If they bothered to ask John if he had any last words, his answer might have been, "It's about time!"

Remember, he's been waiting for a glorious death for almost six decades now. Jesus promised, and brother James got beheaded, and John...waited. Now finally, he's been caught and will go to heaven to see if he does in fact get preferential seating. Whether he expects pain or a martyr's numbness, he can look down and know it's going to be over quickly. Yet that is not what happens. Instead, they lower him into the oil—to no effect.

John is probably as surprised as anyone.

Is this really happening?

While this legend easily could have merged with other miraculous accounts of similar nature, it is said that the crowd that witnessed the incredible miracle immediately converted to Christianity.

What would Darth Domitian be thinking?

Oh, crap!

If this is THE John, the one from the Gospels, then he once got chided by Christ for asking him if he should call fire down from the sky to destroy a Samaritan village that rejected the Gospels! That John.

Tertullian references this part of the tale as if (yawn) he'd heard it a bunch of times:

**"How happy is its church, on which apostles poured forth all their doctrine along with their blood! where Peter endures a passion like his Lord's! where Paul wins his crown in a death like John's where the Apostle John was first plunged, unhurt, into boiling oil, and thence remitted to his island-exile!"**

When I first heard this legend, it was a bit much for me, but then I thought long and hard about Patmos, and after visiting the island, I understood it better. You see, there is no big prison camp system where you bring the world's worst criminals. There was no prison. There was no population. Patmos is a rock with no fresh water source.

What do you do with the Beloved Disciple if you're Domitian? He's far too dangerous to keep in Rome since you now have a coliseum full of new Christians. If you release him, he'll keep preaching. If you put him in a prison, an angel will open a wall OR he'd convert the prison. Sending him to an isolated island where he can do no harm is perfect, but it only makes sense after the boiling oil story. It also makes sense if he is 75 instead of over 90 like other Christ contemporaries would have been. We'll leave him to die on Patmos.

Instead Domitian gets assassinated, and John is released back to Ephesus, with a new message and a new perspective on Christ's martyr promise.

# CHAPTER SEVEN

# TWO OLIVES, SHAKEN AND STIRRED

After John stepped out of the pot of boiling oil, and somewhere on his ride to Patmos, he must have felt a mixture of disappointment, confusion, and exaltation.

Didn't Christ promise John would be a martyr? All of his other colleagues had given their lives as a martyr for Christianity—a sacrifice he was willing to make. Being brought to the Roman Emperor was an opportunity of a lifetime, yet God did not allow it to happen. What gives?

Now around 75, he also knows his life is dwindling down. Will Christ return soon? Sixty years earlier, he'd been given the commission to spread the Gospel to all nations. While Thomas got as far as India, and others died in Africa, nobody has reached China, Australia, or the Americas yet. 99% of his generation, especially those at the Mount of Olives, were now dead

and gone. He was the only one left—meaning Christ would return in his remaining lifetime. So it was going to be a productive
run till he tapped out at 120. Hmm?

Wait...if God spared him in a pot of boiling oil, there must be
something important God's saving him for. John might begin to
realize his request will indeed be granted—but in a much larger
than expected way.

We're not sure how long he lingered on the prison island of
Patmos. Did he evangelize the guards? Do they keep him away
from the guard in solitary confinement? Do they rotate guards
every month of so? John only tells us it was a Sunday when he
finally got his answer.

The Revelation begins, and he literally becomes a secretary
taking notes as a series of speakers deliver important messages
for the existing seven churches around Turkey, future Christians
who'd read the prophecy, and...a specific message for John.

His message?

Angel: Hey, I've got something for you to eat, and then I
need to tell you about the Two Witnesses. You know what I'm
talking about?

John nods. He's a scholar.

Angel: Well, eat up, and I'll review just in case you don't get
it.

## The Two Witnesses: A Primer

In the final days of our fallen world, two mysterious figures
will stand toe-to-toe with (E)vil in a final attempt to gather the
most stubborn of God's children. Filled with the power of the
Holy Spirit, these enigmatic figures will display superhuman

ability in the earth's darkest hour yet will ultimately allow themselves to be martyred (John just perked up) in the blood-stained streets of Jerusalem. Who are these witnesses? Who has God appointed to redeem the unredeemable? The answer to that question might require faith that doesn't belong in this modern age of science and reason. As predicted, the End Times will be filled with scoffers and skeptics that refuse to acknowledge any miracle or sign of God. So too in the time of Christ were the "experts" unable to recognize the signs pointing toward Jesus as the Messiah despite hundreds of scriptural sources unfolding before them. Two thousand years ago, did Jesus Christ, with a twinkle in his eye, lay down the framework for one of His biggest surprises? Why will the world reject and hate these witnesses despite their blatant use of the Holy Spirit? Because the identity of these two men will seem so irrational and illogical that the world will have to view it as a lie rather than trust in the exclusionary will of God.

## **Christianity 101 basics:**

The penalty of sin is death. Yep.
Adam and Eve brought sin into the world. Yep.
Adam and Eve died because they sinned. Yep.
All human beings that sin face the penalty of death. Yep.
Satan made sure all humans fell short in the eyes of God.
(Job nods.)
Jesus came to earth as a mortal human. Yep.
Jesus did not sin, and dying without sin, atoned for our sin.
(Yep=most denominations, right).

These are some basic philosophies found in the Bible. For years, humans have died as a penalty for sinning. It's been a hard and fast rule since Adam and Eve...except for two people in the Old Testament...Enoch and Elijah. The Bible is fairly clear that these men did not experience death but were taken to heaven. Even though human pride would lead us to believe we know a lot about what it means to go to heaven, none of us have a clue. Even enlightened men like Paul mentioned there being different parts to heaven. Thus it is difficult to even understand what it means for Enoch and Elijah to be taken to Heaven while still alive.

Is there some special room just for the two of them?

Are they in some sort of sub-heaven where they can exist while alive?

Are they in the presence of God?

Can a living human even exist in the presence of God?

Are they in the presence of the souls of the dead?

Were there even human souls in heaven prior to Jesus living and dying on earth?

Is this fair, class?

Nerdy kid raises hand: No!

Why? God was very clear that the penalty of sin is death. If Enoch or Elijah had managed to live a sinless life, then what is the need for Christ? NO HUMAN BEING BESIDES CHRIST HAS BEEN SINLESS (ignoring Mary for this one, my Catholic friends)! Despite being righteous men, far better than any of us, these two men still had to have sin. God did not take these men from earth because they were sinless. God did not spare these men death because he loved them more than he loves us. These men might have been taken to Heaven, but it does not mean God spared them death. All sinners owe God a death. Enoch and Elijah were not perfect…but God did have a plan for them, just like he had a plan for John. They were special, but not so special that they were above death.

## Witness #1: Enoch

Many modern experts believe the two witnesses will be Moses and Elijah. After all, the spirits of these two men appeared to Christ during the Transfiguration. The biggest problem I have with this theory is that Moses is quite dead. His body is also quite decayed by now. The two witnesses appear prior to the resurrection of the dead. Besides, Moses has already paid the price of sin. He's had his death. The two witnesses in Revelations are mortal men that will be slain by evil men. During the Transfiguration, Moses was a spirit that visited Jesus. Despite being an important figure in the Bible, Moses had done his part. The witnesses will be two men that have not died yet.

Despite the fact that there are only two human beings in the Old Testament that did not experience death, very little is known about Enoch. Enoch was born 622 years after Adam began to die (I'm not sure how long he existed before becoming mortal). He was the seventh generation after Adam, who was still alive when Enoch was born. In this pre-flood world, all the patriarchs were living to an average of 900 years. By the seventh generation, the world of man had to be flourishing. While the descendants of Cain and Seth filled the earth, the patriarchs remained faithful to God.

**[Genesis 5:21]: And Enoch lived sixty and five years, and begat Methuselah: [22]And Enoch walked with God after he begat Methuselah three hundred years, and begat sons and daughters: [23] And all the days of Enoch were three hundred sixty and five years: [24] And Enoch walked with God: and he was not; for God took him.**

That is all we get (Unless you're from the Ethiopian Church). Of course, the abstract words in that passage was "walked" with God. What does it mean to walk with God? Does it connote closeness with God? What happened when Enoch walked with God? The book of Hebrews also briefly mentions Enoch.

**[Hebrews 11:5]: By faith Enoch was translated that he should not see death; and was not found, because God had translated him: for before his translation he had this testimony, that he pleased God. [6 ]But without faith it is impossible to please him: for he that cometh to God must believe that he is, and that he is a rewarder of them that diligently seek him.**

Faith seems to be a large part of the equation, but then again, the writer of Hebrews mentions the faith of Noah, Abraham, Sara, and others. Did any of them go right to heaven or walk with God? Perhaps walking with God means something else. Perhaps it has something to do with the testimony of Enoch. What is this testimony? Unfortunately, we don't get any words from Enoch in the book of Genesis. Jude, a brother/cousin of Christ, gives us a little insight into Enoch.

**[Jude 1:14] And Enoch also, the seventh from Adam, prophesied of these, saying, Behold, the Lord cometh with ten thousands of his saints, 15 To execute judgment upon all, and to convince all that are ungodly among them of all their**

**ungodly deeds which they have ungodly committed, and of all their hard speeches which ungodly sinners have spoken against him.**

Jude quoted Enoch. But where did that information come from? In Jude 6 and 13, it refers to the fallen angels and/or Nephilim found before the flood. How did Jude know about this stuff? In the time of Christ, one of the known books was the Book of Enoch. Although a definitive version of this book did not exist when the Bible was being formed, early Christians still knew these stories. In the Book of Enoch, Enoch was vividly portrayed as a prophet that not only predicted the impending flood but also the end of the world (2 Peter 3:7). Walking with God is the equivalent of being a prophet of God. He was born with a gift. Perhaps he was the first prophet. Perhaps he will be the last.

Is Enoch one of the witnesses? Yes, that would make a lot of sense. In the past 150 years, the greatest contributor to the apostasy (falling away) of Christianity has been the absolute interpretation of Genesis and the age of the earth. The 6K folks cannot believe the 6 Billion folks, and the 6 Billion folks cannot believe the 6K folks—division! You can twist and contort (on either sides) to make it the way you want it be read, but neither side has 100% absolute certainty. But Enoch? Enoch was there!

Enoch would be a perfect candidate to speak to these hard-hearted folks (on both sides, too). Remember, these witnesses will not be speaking to a world of Christians. Most Christians will be absent through either natural disaster or divine rapture. (Since we all owe a death for sin, perhaps the Christians will be the victims of the 5th and 6th seals). The two witnesses will be speaking to a world jaded by disaster and stubborn skepticism. Their mission—to bring in the last of the scoffers into God's family. Since the witnesses will be located in Jerusalem, they will undoubtedly be speaking to Jews, God's chosen people. Think of what Enoch has seen…

He's been to Heaven

He's seen Christ pre-incarnate

He's seen Christ return to Heaven as a purified man.

He's known Adam

He's seen how the Pre-flood world works

He's received a prophecy of a worldwide flood

He's received a prophecy of a fire that scours the world.

He's walked with God.

Enoch was not taken to Heaven to avoid death. In Revelation, the two witnesses will clearly die a mortal death. They will bleed because they are flesh and blood. If my theory is correct, Enoch does owe God a death, but his sentence has been stayed. His death is still coming. He will die on the streets of Jerusalem.

So does that mean Enoch is still alive and 6,000 years old? I suppose it does. We do not have any stories of Enoch coming back down to earth and dying. How does he stay alive? I suppose if he is physically in Heaven, things don't have to operate by the law of physics. I suppose he could be in some sort of suspended animation that keeps him from aging. Maybe Heaven preserves his human body. But he still is flesh and bone, so maybe there are other answers to how he still exists. I like to believe he's been learning this whole time. Think of the wisdom this man would hold. What wouldn't he know? He'd have every answer for every scoffer—be it Christian or Atheist.

# Elijah the Witness?

Unlike Enoch, there are many stories about Elijah. By looking only at the Old Testament, it would seem pretty easy to match Elijah with Enoch as the second witness. In Revelation 11:5, it tells that the two witnesses will be able to send fire from their mouth to consume anyone trying to harm them. In 1 Kings 18:38, Elijah called the fires of God to defeat his enemies. In fact, there are not many prophets that can rival the power of this mighty man. Let's review Elijah's feats:

1 Kings 17:1-8 Elijah proclaims a drought.

1 Kings 17:8-16 Miraculous replenishing of food.

1 Kings 17:17-24 Elijah asks God to restore life to a boy.

1 Kings 18 Elijah slaughters the priests of Baal.

1 Kings 19 Elijah eats a cake made by the Angel of the Lord.

1 Kings 19 Elijah visits Mt. Horeb (Sinai).

1 Kings 20-22 Elijah warns the wicked.

2 Kings 2 Elijah ascends to Heaven.

2 Kings 2 Elisha continues the fight.

2 Kings 13 Elisha dies.

Obviously, Elijah was a powerful man of God. He also was a killer. He killed men. Even though they were evil men, he still sinned and owes God a death. But what a fit for the second witness! Perhaps the most convincing factor in being a witness is his sojourn to Mt. Horeb in chapter 19. Elijah did not view himself as perfect, and even asks for his death for being no better than his fathers. Then he has a visitor. Some think that the Angel of the Lord is not just an ordinary angel but the preincarnate Christ. Now that really qualifies him as a witness. He's been chosen by Christ himself. At this meeting with the Angel of the Lord, he is given cake. This angel cake sustained him on a walk to Mt. Horeb, which is also known as Mt. Sinai. This is the same mountain where Moses met with God and received the Ten Commandments.

Whether Mt. Horeb is Mt. Jabal Musa, Jabal al Lawz, or Mystery Mountain C, it is still a long walk without food or water for 40 days. This was a special food. In fact, I believe it could be manna. With manna in his belly, Elijah was easily sustained on this walk. Once he got to Mt. Horeb, he entered the sacred cave of God where he conversed with the Almighty. In God's presence, Elijah wrapped his mantle around his body to protect him from God's holy presence. Much later, Elijah took his apprentice Elisha with him to witness his ascension to Heaven. A chariot of fire came down and took Elijah up into Heaven. Elisha saw all of this and told others. In fact, Elijah made such a lasting impact on the Jewish people, that many years later, the prophet Malachi made a prophecy concerning the prophet.

**[Malachi 4:5] Behold, I will send you Elijah the prophet before the coming of the great and dreadful day of the LORD: [6 ]And he shall turn the heart of the fathers to the children, and the heart of the children to their fathers, lest I come and smite the earth with a curse.**

Elijah wasn't going to just stay in Heaven…he was coming back. Now, many experts take the easy path and say all this adds up to make Elijah the second witness. This verse from Malachi almost seals the deal…almost. To us, the great and dreadful day of the Lord sounds like Revelation. To Malachi, this also could have meant the coming of Christ as a man. In fact, there are many problems with Elijah being the second witness. The biggest problem comes from the mouth of Christ himself.

## Elijah the Witness, Cross-examined

Perhaps the most abstract verse from the Bible is Second Kings 2:9. In this verse, Elisha asks for a "double portion" of Elijah's spirit. What? Elisha knew his mentor was leaving. Elisha would now be the leading man in the fight against evil. He probably worried he didn't have enough power to sustain the cause. But rather than simply asking for his own strength as Joshua had after Moses left, Elisha asked for Elijah's spirit.

What does that mean?

We do not even understand how our own soul works. We definitely do not understand how Elijah's powerful soul works. But the request is granted. Elijah isn't even sure if it is possible or if it'll work. But as soon as Elijah goes to Heaven, it does happen. He gets a part of Elijah's spirit. It would be easier to just think that Elisha was given more power by the Holy Spirit or God, but that is not how this scene is described. From that moment the mantle fell on him, Elisha was more than he once was. Perhaps the easiest way to understand this could be from a classic piece of pop culture. Just as Obi Wan Kenobi guided Luke Skywalker in spirit, perhaps part of Elijah's soul guided Elisha. Or perhaps it is even more explicit than that. What if Elijah could divide his soul? Perhaps part of his soul continued to exist with his physical body in Heaven while the other part of his soul went down to Elisha. Isn't that what this scene describes? Who are we to know what God can or can't do? Even Elijah wasn't sure this could happen, but it seems that it did.

Now, from this moment, Elisha really started to act just like Elijah. He divided the river Jordan just as Elijah had done earlier. He healed, he struck wicked youths dead out of anger, he raised a child from death. Now I do not believe Elijah possessed Elisha and took him over, but what if two spirits could inhabit a human body. It works for demons, why not for the good guys? When Elisha dies in Chapter 13, things are definitely not normal. When a dead man touched the bones of Elisha, the dead man was brought back to life. One thing is clear…Elisha died. So what happened to the spirit of Elijah? The rest of his spirit was in Heaven still with his body. Did he half die? Can such a thing be so?

## The Return of Elijah

One thing is indisputable…Elijah was coming back. Malachi knew this. But how? No one has ever come back before. Enoch hadn't. What was going to happen to Elijah? The Jews probably expected thunder, lightning, and earthquakes when Elijah returned. Regardless of the manner of his return, the purpose of his return is clear. Elijah is to prepare the people to be ready to listen to Christ so that Christ doesn't condemn the world.

Wait a second?!

Aren't the witnesses there to gather up the lost because the world is already being destroyed? Armageddon is the end. The witnesses are the last chance. They are not there to prepare and nourish. They are there to throw life preservers to the last converts. The purpose described in Malachi does not match the purpose described for the two witnesses.

But Elijah is coming back, right?

According to Christ, everyone missed it. It even happened prior to Christ's death.

How did we miss that? It doesn't say anything about Elijah in the New Testament, does it? Oh wait, it does.

An angel came to visit a couple named Zacharias and Elizabeth. The angel told the couple that they would give birth to a very special child. This child would not act or behave like other children. Even in the womb of Elizabeth, the child recognized and understood that Mary was pregnant with the Messiah. How could a regular human baby know so much? Well perhaps he'd been prepared for the past few hundred years in Heaven. Perhaps this child already knew the Spirit of Jesus Christ before he recognized the human. Or maybe this child came with a little extra. Isn't that what the angel was preparing them for?

Luke spelled it out.

**Luke 1:17 And he will go on before the Lord in the spirit and power of Elijah, to turn the hearts of the fathers to their children and the disobedient to the wisdom of the righteous— to make ready a people prepared for the Lord.**

Let's get this straight. This child has a direct connection to the verse from Malachi. This child will fulfill Malachi. Could it be that the child will be given the second half of Elijah just like Elisha had been given the first half?

This child grew up to be John the Baptist. In this manner, he definitely fulfilled the prophecy of preparing the way for Christ. Unlike Christ, the Jews warmly embraced the preaching of John and quickly embraced him as a prophet of God. While we do not have any stories of his childhood, we do know that he shared many similarities with Elijah that did not go unnoticed by the leaders of the church.

He dressed in animal skins like Elijah

He ate locust and honey like Elijah

He inspired fear and awe like Elijah

He openly condemned the king of Judea like Elijah

He knew he'd been sent to prepare the way for Christ.

The priests and the Levites knew something was up:

**[John 1:21) And they asked him, "what then? Are you Elijah?" He said, "I am not."**

I guess that wraps it up. John denied it. He said he is not Elijah. Unfortunately, John probably had some very good reason for saying this. What if he had said he was Elijah? The country would have exploded with faux-religious fervor. No one would have listened to him. John's mission was to prepare the way. Answering 'yes' would have undone his message. It was Jesus that explained things better.

**[Matthew 11:7] And as they departed, Jesus began to say unto the multitudes concerning John, What went ye out into the wilderness to see? A reed shaken with the wind? [8] But what went ye out for to see? A man clothed in soft raiment? behold, they that wear soft clothing are in kings' houses. [9] But what went ye out for to see? A prophet? yea, I say unto you, and more than a prophet. [10] For this is he, of whom it is written, Behold, I send my messenger before thy face, which shall prepare thy way before thee.**
**[11] Verily I say unto you, Among them that are born of women there hath not risen a greater than John the Baptist: notwithstanding he that is least in the kingdom of heaven is greater than he. [12] And from the days of John the Baptist**

**until now the kingdom of heaven suffereth violence, and the violent take it by force. [13] For all the prophets and the law prophesied until John. [14] And if ye will receive it, this is Elias, which was for to come. [15] He that hath ears to hear, let him hear.**

There we have it. Jesus tried his best to spell it out for us. John is more than a prophet. He is the fulfillment of prophecy. He is Elijah (Elias). Who do we believe? John or Jesus. I'll go with Jesus. Jesus didn't expect people to get it. It is an abstract concept. This isn't the only place we have a connection between John the Baptist and Elijah. **Matthew 17** describes the transfiguration of Jesus on the mountain. Jesus took Peter, James, and John to this high mountain. On the mountain, Moses and Elijah appeared to Jesus. We all know that Moses was dead. What about Elijah? Coincidentally, John the Baptist had just been executed. If part of his soul had died with Elisha and part of his soul died with John the Baptist, it seems Elijah had given God his death. That is why Elijah was now able to meet with Jesus. This wasn't John the Baptist because Jesus hardly knew this man. Jesus did know Elijah from Elijah's time in heaven. They both went down about the same time. They shared and understood the mission. Heading into his darkest hour, Jesus needed advice and inspiration from both Moses and Elijah.

Seeing Elijah, the disciples wondered if the Malachi prophecy had been wrong. They knew the Son of God was Jesus. They also recognized Elijah. But they knew Elijah was supposed to return prior to the Messiah. Well the Messiah had come and they hadn't seen Elijah return to earth in physical form. John the Baptist and Elijah must not have looked alike.

Jesus explains this in

**[Matthew 17:10]: And his disciples asked him, saying, Why then say the scribes that Elias must first come? [11] And Jesus answered and said unto them, Elias truly shall first come, and restore all things. [12] But I say unto you, That Elias is come already, and they knew him not, but have done unto him whatsoever they listed. Likewise shall also the Son of man suffer of them. [13] Then the disciples understood that he spake unto them of John the Baptist.**

Elijah has come already. He came as John the Baptist. No one understood. We can clearly see that John=Elijah when Jesus said that they did to Elijah whatever they wished. John the Baptist was beheaded by his own people. When on earth, Elijah was not killed by anyone. Jesus said he'd die like Elijah died. Elijah had died with John the Baptist. Jesus knew John and Elijah were one and the same.

This leaves us with one slight problem. If Elijah gave God his owed death, then who is the second witness? Ironically, Elijah did more than baptize people. He prepared the way for Christ by preparing the ultimate disciple. This disciple was not only trained and educated to be a disciple of Christ by Elijah, he was trained to be the second witness. The disciple of John the Baptist was John the son of Zebedee.

## John the Witness

Just the fact that John was given the full vision of the End Times is enough to qualify him for the title of Beloved Disciple. But with all the visuals and symbolism of Revelation, it is easy to lose sight of the fact that John is sitting there speaking with Christ and angels. He is an active witness for what is going to unfold. Aside from being told to write all these things down for Christians to read for the next 2,000 years, I believe there is another purpose for John to be given this vision.

After all, dozens of Old Testament prophets and even some disciples were given the rundown on what would happen. Jesus's simple account in Matthew, Mark, and Luke is enough for any Christian to understand and not miss it. The Revelation of John hasn't even been that helpful to Church leaders over the past 2,000 years. If anything, it's the black sheep of the Bible that is either confused or ignored.

Why was John given all those details? Because he was going to be an active participant in the story. He'd be groomed as no other human had been groomed. Enoch got to walk with God. John got to walk with Jesus and get taught by John the Baptist and the Virgin Mary. Any person that could write could have been given this prophecy. John was given Revelation because he had been groomed to be the second witness. Even as Revelation was given to him, he didn't know he was about to be chosen as the second witness.

On the Mount of Olives, Jesus originally gave John a list of things that would happen before Judgment Day arrives. John also understood now that these things would happen before he received his martyr's death. Except for the destruction of Jerusalem, which had already happened 25 years earlier, none of the other signs had happened and now John was reaching 75 years. On Patmos, Jesus again reviews these same prophecies, except in greater detail. Revelation 1-7 is a review of what he learned on the Mount of Olives.

Then Jesus begins giving John new information, which of course, John knows must happen shortly before his own death. In fact, many scholars believe the trumpet blasts of Revelation 8 will happen in quick succession. I believe the trumpet blasts will occur while John is in Jerusalem acting as the second witness along with Enoch. That is why these details were not given in the gospels. John essentially is given all the details to look for BEFORE he has to do his duty.

Revelation 9 & 10 describe a world in which the Christians have already been raptured. The Rapture could occur through either natural deaths in the great earthquake of the 6th seal OR through some passive yet miraculous "Poof" and disappearance of all Christians on the face of the earth. Since Revelation discusses a cynical world of nonbelievers, the death theory seems easier for the scoffers to fathom without acknowledging the authority of God (sorry Jerry Jenkins!) After all, I know I've sinned and I owe God a death. I don't deserve a cop-out magical, painless Poof. 21st century Christians definitely have sinned enough to owe God a death. What arrogance to think we just get to have a free ride to Heaven because we happened to live at the end! If I'm still around after seal four, I'll gladly face the Earthquake and big explosion.

After the Christians are gathered up, John is shown that the surviving humans are suddenly in the middle between a fight between Good and Evil. Demons, Apollyon, and Fallen Angels are released upon humanity. With the Christians gone and the Antichrist about to take power, there are only two forces of Good to defend all the remaining sinners that still can have a part of God's eternal kingdom…the Two Witnesses.

Revelation 10 and 11 discuss the two witnesses. In fact, I wish when they broke the Bible into chapters and verses, they'd grouped 10 & 11 together. John didn't write them in chapters and verses. I think part of the reason John is not seen as one witness is simply because of the chapter break. All this time, John has been carefully watching all the images shown to him by Christ and the Angels concerning the End Times. In Chapter 10, however, something different happens. There is a break in the visualization that had shown John 2,000 years into the future. Suddenly, John is right back in Patmos in the year 95:

**[Revelation 10:1]: And I saw another mighty angel come down from heaven, clothed with a cloud: and a rainbow was upon his head, and his face was as it were the sun, and his feet as pillars of fire: [2 ]And he had in his hand a little book open: and he set his right foot upon the sea, and his left foot on the earth, [3] And cried with a loud voice, as when a lion roareth: and when he had cried, seven thunders uttered their voices. [4 ] And when the seven thunders had uttered their voices, I was about to write: and I heard a voice from heaven saying unto me, Seal up those things which the seven thunders uttered, and write them not. [5 ]And the angel which I saw stand upon the sea and upon the earth lifted up his hand to heaven, [6 ]And sware by him that liveth for ever and ever, who created heaven, and the things that therein are, and the earth, and the things that therein are, and the sea, and the things which are therein, that there should be time no longer: [7 ]But in the days of the voice of the seventh angel, when he shall begin to sound, the mystery of God should be finished, as he hath declared to his servants the prophets.**

**[8 ]And the voice which I heard from heaven spake unto me again, and said, Go and take the little book which is open in the hand of the angel which standeth upon the sea and upon**

the earth. [9]And I went unto the angel, and said unto him, Give me the little book. And he said unto me, Take it, and eat it up; and it shall make thy belly bitter, but it shall be in thy mouth sweet as honey. [10] And I took the little book out of the angel's hand, and ate it up; and it was in my mouth sweet as honey: and as soon as I had eaten it, my belly was bitter. [11] And he said unto me, Thou must prophesy again before many peoples, and nations, and tongues, and kings.

John was told something important, but he was also told not to write it down. Then what was the point? It obviously wasn't an accident. He was meant to hear it, but NOT to give it to us in his book of Revelation. Then who is the message for? The message is for the post-rapture humans. John was given a message not intended for regular Christians otherwise he would have written it. When he stands in Jerusalem, he will then speak those things the seven thunders told him to say. (Remember, John's nickname is "Son of Thunder.")

The angel continues this timeout in prophecy to drop the rest of the message:

[Revelation 11:1]: And there was given me a reed like unto a rod: and the angel stood, saying, Rise, and measure the temple of God, and the altar, and them that worship therein. [2] But the court which is without the temple leave out, and measure it not; for it is given unto the Gentiles: and the holy city shall they tread under foot forty and two months. [3]And I will give power unto my two witnesses, and they shall prophesy a thousand two hundred and threescore days, clothed in sackcloth. [4] These are the two olive trees, and the two candlesticks standing before the God of the earth. [5] And if any man will hurt them, fire proceedeth out of their mouth, and devoureth their enemies: and if any man will hurt them,

**he must in this manner be killed. [6] These have power to shut heaven, that it rain not in the days of their prophecy: and have power over waters to turn them to blood, and to smite the earth with all plagues, as often as they will.**

## Counting Easter Eggs

I'm going to have to skip over a bunch of details in those two passages, which I'll save for the next chapter. This chapter is about the two witnesses. Focus.

Notice how the conversation about the End Times suddenly shifts to talk about the Temple. In the year 95, the Temple had already been leveled (again) for 25 years. It wasn't coming back. It hasn't come back. In this vision, however, John is told to get specific measurements for the temple. John literally was given a rod, a big ruler. The angel stood there with his arms crossed while John measured the...hologram. What is John measuring? I say hologram because it is either a portal to the past or a projection of the future. Either way, that's some real trippy Matrix stuff going on. John time-traveled?

As John is dutifully measuring the "virtual" Temple, which would have taken quite a while if it was to scale, he would have had time to ponder what the angel just said to him. Today, the kids call clues in movies "Easter eggs." Marvel movies are notorious for leaving visual clues about stuff that is coming in the next phase of movies. Marvel geeks will watch the movie a dozen times before these clues pop out. For John, he was given several Biblical Easter eggs in the previous passage, so as he was measuring, he might have found a couple. If not, then these clues were meant for us.

# Egg #1: Olive Trees

John walked in Temple 2.0. Solomon's Temple 1.0 was knocked down by the Babylonians centuries earlier, and after the exile in Babylon, Jews were allowed to return to Jerusalem to begin rebuilding it...Temple 2.0. Now, I have some pretty gnarly theories about Solomon that are not appropriate for this chapter/book, but rebuilding Temple 2.0 was a MAJOR undertaking, which needed some divine help. The books of Ezra and Nehemiah discuss this, which certainly went through John's mind at some time. Yet the Easter Egg he would have noticed was the symbolism of what he was just shown. It matches Zechariah, who wrote.

**[Zechariah 4:1] And the angel that talked with me came again, and waked me, as a man that is wakened out of his sleep, [2] And said unto me, What seest thou? And I said, I have looked, and behold a candlestick all of gold, with a bowl upon the top of it, and his seven lamps thereon, and seven pipes to the seven lamps, which are upon the top thereof: [3] And two olive trees by it, one upon the right side of the bowl, and the other upon the left side thereof. [4] So I answered and spake to the angel that talked with me, saying, What are these, my lord? [5] Then the angel that talked with me answered and said unto me, Knowest thou not what these be? And I said, No, my lord. [6] Then he answered and spake unto me, saying, This is the word of the LORD unto Zerubbabel, saying, Not by might, nor by power, but by my spirit, saith the LORD of hosts. [7] Who art thou, O great mountain? before Zerubbabel thou shalt become a plain: and he shall bring forth the headstone thereof with shoutings, crying, Grace, grace unto it.**
**[8] Moreover the word of the LORD came unto me, saying, [9] The hands of Zerubbabel have laid the foundation of this**

**house; his hands shall also finish it; and thou shalt know that the LORD of hosts hath sent me unto you. [10] For who hath despised the day of small things? for they shall rejoice, and shall see the plummet in the hand of Zerubbabel with those seven; they are the eyes of the LORD, which run to and fro through the whole earth.**

**[11] Then answered I, and said unto him, What are these two olive trees upon the right side of the candlestick and upon the left side thereof? [12] And I answered again, and said unto him, What be these two olive branches which through the two golden pipes empty the golden oil out of themselves? [13] And he answered me and said, Knowest thou not what these be? And I said, No, my lord. [14] then said he, These are the two anointed ones, that stand by the Lord of the whole earth.**

So John was just told to get a measurement of the Temple, and both the two olive trees seem to match the idea of the two witnesses.

Now, after this vision, which Ezra also records, two men, Jeshua (not the same) and Zerubbabal begin building Temple 2.0. These guys were the builders. The two olive trees were not specified as them. So who was the architect?

## Egg #2: The Bronze Architect

Ezekiel adds some insight.

**[Ezekiel 40:2] In the visions of God brought me into the land of Israel, and set me upon a very high mountain, by which was as the frame of a city on the south. [3] And he brought me thither, and, behold, there was a man, whose appearance was like the appearance of brass, with a line of flax in his hand, and a measuring reed; and he stood in the gate. [4] And the man said**

**unto me, Son of man, behold with thine eyes, and hear with thine ears, and set thine heart upon all that I shall shew thee; for to the intent that I might shew them unto thee art thou brought hither: declare all that thou seest to the house of Israel.**

So Ezekiel gets the building spec's from a guy with a measuring rod. Huh? One story involves two olive trees=witnesses. The other story involves a dude with a measuring stick. To rebuild the temple, you need the two witnesses. And who has the measurements?

Um, John.

Although I'm not privy to John's complexion, I would like to point out right now that he's eaten the angel food we'll be discussing in the next chapter.

## Egg #3: The Daniel Clock

Forty-two months. That's how long the two witnesses get to preach in their "safe zone" of the Temple, which John just measured. Why such a specific time? Where else is such a time mentioned?

The final chapter of Daniel, which had PLENTY of End Times talk already, especially about beasts, has several parallels to what John has experienced.

It starts by talking about how rough the last days will be, but that the dead will rise, so...yay! Daniel is warned that even though he's seen the End Times, that he can't give a full disclosure of what is to come, and like John, has to "seal" things up, which in Daniel's account is a book instead of his lips (remember this sealed book for next chapter). Did Daniel have any connections to our Easter eggs?

> **[Daniel 12:5] Then I Daniel looked, and, behold, there stood other two, the one on this side of the bank of the river, and the other on that side of the bank of the river. [6]And one said to the man clothed in linen, which was upon the waters of the river, How long shall it be to the end of these wonders? [7] And I heard the man clothed in linen, which was upon the waters of the river, when he held up his right hand and his left hand unto heaven, and sware by him that liveth for ever that it shall be for a time, times, and an half; and when he shall have accomplished to scatter the power of the holy people, all these things shall be finished. [8] And I heard, but I understood not: then said I, O my Lord, what shall be the end of these things? [9] And he said, Go thy way, Daniel: for the words are closed up and sealed till the time of the end. [10] Many shall be purified, and made white, and tried; but the wicked shall do wickedly: and none of the wicked shall understand; but the wise shall understand. [11] And from the time that the daily sacrifice shall be taken away, and the abomination that maketh desolate set up, there shall be a thousand two hundred and ninety days. [12] Blessed is he that waiteth, and cometh to the thousand three hundred and five and thirty days. [13] But go thou thy way till the end be: for thou shalt rest, and stand in thy lot at the end of the days.**

While not 42 months, Daniel 12 has 3 sets of times, doesn't it? A vague time, and two specific times (1290 and 1335 days). Hmm? Who would need to know such things about the final years? A witness!

And the imagery! Two dudes=2 witnesses=2 olive trees. Daniel opens some portal and begins listening:

River Bank Dude: When's the End?

Floating Dude: Vague answer

For John, who stood on a river bank to see Jesus baptized, this scene has personal imagery for him, doesn't it? And the content? Check out Mark 13, which is set at the Mount of Olives where Jesus gives four of his guys the End Times talk:

**[Mark 13:3] And as he sat upon the mount of Olives over against the temple, Peter and James and John and Andrew asked him privately, [4] Tell us, when shall these things be? and what shall be the sign when all these things shall be fulfilled?**

John=River Bank Dude

Jesus=Floating Dude

Yes, John most likely asked the exact same question as the River Bank Dude. And guess what, Jesus gives a vague answer about no one but God knowing the exact when, because, yada, yada, yada, Seven Seals, stuff you don't understand yet, I haven't died, so...yeah, only God knows! So did Daniel peep into the future to see John ask Jesus this question on the Mount of Olives? Wow...sneaky prophet. This could also be a portal to the "secret stuff" that John learns and is told to keep it quiet. That fits too. Either way, Daniel is possibly using his Infinity Stone prophetic abilities to get answers from the future, isn't he? Strange stuff.

Well, it gets stranger. Daniel interrupts the vision by throwing out his own question, and is promptly told by His Lord to go away (back to the past). Yet Daniel insists, and the Lordly Floating Figure tells him that the Abomination of Desolation will start a countdown, which will have VERY specific days to the end.

Well, guess what else John asked:

**[Matt 24:15 When ye therefore shall see the abomination of desolation, spoken of by Daniel the prophet, stand in the holy place, (whoso readeth, let him understand:)...]**

Yep, John got the same clue as Daniel, which is why I think they might have known each other from the...portal? If Daniel could see the two witnesses, couldn't THEY see Daniel? Strange stuff indeed.

## Egg #4: Fire

For 3 ½ years, the Two Witnesses (JLW theory=John and Enoch) will preach upon the ruins of the Temple. I believe their testimony begins after the 6th seal. That is when John will assume his position as witness. Remember, it will be an evil world void of most Christians. It is also a world filled with demons. Speaking truth in all this darkness will be John and Enoch. John will speak what the Seven Thunders told him. No one can stop them, either. They will have unbelievable power. In fact, it sounds as if Jesus might have promised this power to John years ago.

**[Luke 9:51] And it came to pass, when the time was come that he should be received up, he steadfastly set his face to go to Jerusalem, [52] And sent messengers before his face: and they went, and entered into a village of the Samaritans, to make ready for him. [53] And they did not receive him, because his face was as though he would go to Jerusalem. [54] And when his disciples James and John saw this, they said, Lord, wilt**

**thou that we command fire to come down from heaven, and consume them, even as Elias did? [55] But he turned, and rebuked them, and said, Ye know not what manner of spirit ye are of. 56 For the Son of man is not come to destroy men's lives, but to save them. And they went to another village.**

Somewhere along the way, John and James knew they had supernatural powers. The most frightening part of this question is that Jesus knew they could have destroyed the village. Jesus made them powerful and zealous, but John had to learn compassion. As a witness, he will speak words in hopes of persuading sinners to let Christ into their hearts. As defense, these witnesses will wield incredible powers for defense. Remember, John had asked Jesus to let him be a martyr.

Could there be another reason for measuring the temple? Certainly. Many scholars believe that before the End Times can happen, the Temple must be rebuilt. If it is rebuilt, I know somebody that will know how to build it!

Does the temple need to be rebuilt? I guess it depends on your interpretation of Daniel. If it doesn't, I still think I know what John is being told. The two witnesses will have a bubble of protection around them. Perhaps this bubble will only exist where the temple once stood. Right now, a Muslim Temple stands on the ruins of the temple. Perhaps the Gentiles already are at the temple.

John is shown the future all the way up until the Sixth Trumpet. Then an angel shows up, whispers in John's ear, and tells him that everything will be said before the seventh trumpet. The seventh trumpet will be blown right after the witnesses die. The seven thunders told John the mysteries of God to be shared after the sixth seal. How can anybody but John know what that is? But how can John last until then? It's not physically possible!

(Unless...what exactly did John eat?)

# CHAPTER EIGHT

# PINKY SWEAR

While modern Christianity seems content to sell the Two Witnesses as Moses and Elijah, or Enoch and Elijah, or Daniel and Ezekiel, or...(insert your theory here), I have a hard time getting past what happens in Revelation 10 & 11. In the middle of the End Times preview, an angel shows up, calls a time-out, gives John some food, makes him measure a virtual temple, talks about the Two Witnesses, jumps into a BIG flashback about Satan trying to murder Jesus (back in the day), and then continues the timeline in Chapter 13 with the Antichrist showing up.

Whew...

It was some great exposition and backstory, but as a creative writing instructor, TELLING is a writing no-no. You don't stop the suspense to give backstory. The earth was just rocked with the biggest earthquake ever experienced. Heck, the Rapture just happened. It was a great cliffhanger, so tell us what happens next, Mr. Angel. Instead, we have three chapters of backstory.

## The Flashback

While the opening chapters are mostly meant for the churches in 95 A.D., and the majority of the other chapters are for Christians in the future, these three chapters are specifically for John.

Do you remember when Mary Magdalene ran back to the disciples to tell them about Christ rising from the tomb? John does. He and Peter took off running for the tomb (John got there first), only to find it empty.

Where did he (Jesus) go?

It was a question John had to ponder the rest of Easter, possibly as he was walking home, and certainly when Jesus showed up in the upper room to show everybody (except Thomas) his proof of his resurrection. Where had Jesus gone? Where was he for most of that day?

Take a look at Chapter 12 and convince me it's not a flashback to Easter. The bloody lamb! Taking the seal! Jesus is showing John what he did between the Mary Magdalene sighting (don't touch, haven't gone to Heaven yet) to his appearance in the Upper Room (go ahead and touch, I'm real). It's like this section is just for John's understanding.

Another question John asked was: When will the End Times happen?

He just got his answer in a very vague way. My interpretation of the answer is that on Easter morning, Jesus the bloody lamb received the sealed scroll, which began the process. You can't read the scroll until all seven seals are opened, right? While Jesus gave John the Cliff Notes of what was on the scroll, Christ could not give him a specific time (only God knows). YET...when the last two seals are cracked, I can give you specific days, including the 1260 days of the Two Witnesses preaching in Jerusalem (and a reference to the other two timelines given to Daniel). Answered (kinda).

Another question that John must've wanted was: When will I die?

Jesus promised James and John they'd die a martyr's death, and in the year 95 AD, every disciple had already died, including his beheaded-brother James. Do you remember how Jesus said "this" generation would not die until all these things (seals 1-7 stuff) took place. Well, John is the last man standing, and just when he got to the part about a possible death, we got our big timeout for chapters 10-13. This question has festered in his mind for quite awhile. It was first uttered six decades earlier at Galilee.

## Christ's Crystal Ball

In previous chapters, I've brought up a bunch of passages where Jesus made promises involving John. These promises ranged from being a martyr to the conditions of the End Times beginning. Yet there was another bizarre moment often lost in Sunday sermons.

The scene involves Peter and John (who walk around a lot together after the crucifixion). This scene happens after the tomb, road to Emmaus, and wound inspection. Remember how Thomas was gone for the wound inspection get-together? Well, he was the only one who actually listened to Jesus and left for Galilee (Matt 26:32/Mark 14:28). He missed the party because he listened to Christ's promise about showing up in Galilee.

Even the angels around the tomb chided the others for not going to Galilee. Even when Mary Magdalene reached for His feet, Christ brought up Galilee. Jesus had promised.

So they went to Galilee (Matt 28:16) to find Thomas and get the promised Jesus sighting (who did show up). While they were up north (and done poking Jesus like a doughboy), there is another Jesus-sighting chronicled by John. Most preachers will focus on the "restoration" of Peter, since it is a message all sinners and doubters understand so well. It's a very cool moment right until Peter starts thinking about the End Times trigger.

What trigger?

Remember how Jesus said specifically to the guys on the Mount of Olives about "this" generation not dying until Jesus comes again (aka...End Times, Armageddon, Apocalypse, Judgment Day). Peter was just told to spread the Gospel to all nations (the first condition/seal?), and his mind immediately went to: how long will this take?

Yes, he's now restored.

Yes, he has a purpose.

But...I'm getting up there. I'm an aging married man and the earth is pretty big. Is Jesus saying that I'll live long enough to get to Tahiti? Oh wait, John is much younger than me...

Sensing this, Jesus said to Peter (with John standing there):

**[John 21:18] Verily, verily, I say unto thee, When thou wast young, thou girdedst thyself, and walkedst whither thou wouldest: but when thou shalt be old, thou shalt stretch forth thy hands, and another shall gird thee, and carry thee whither thou wouldest not. [19] This spake he, signifying by what death he should glorify God. And when he had spoken this, he saith unto him, Follow me.**

**[20] Then Peter, turning about, seeth the disciple whom Jesus loved following; which also leaned on his breast at supper, and said, Lord, which is he that betrayeth thee? [21] Peter seeing him saith to Jesus, Lord, and what shall this man do? [22] Jesus saith unto him, If I will that he tarry till I come, what is that to thee? follow thou me.**

We will be returning to this anecdote in a later chapter, especially for the discussion of John calling himself "the Beloved Disciple." John clarifies that he's the guy who asked the question about Judas, that he was the leaner, and that he was there with Peter when this happened at Galilee. Got it? Good.

Now, let's break down what happened from Peter's POV.

- He'd denied Jesus three times.
- Back in Judea, he didn't get to set things right.
- Back in Galilee, he still didn't get to set thing right.
- Now, while fishing, Jesus shows up again just to set things right.
- Jesus echoes the three denials by giving him three challenges.
- Sweet. (But not enough for Peter)
- Peter wonders about the promise of "spreading the Gospel    to all nations.
- Which Jesus picks up on…
- So Jesus gave a harsh prophecy of Peter's crucifixion death.
- Harsh!

For John, who lives six more decades to the year 95 AD, he must think of this moment as he receives everything said in chapters 10-12 (even the stuff he is told not to write). Like Peter, he must be wondering about his death triggering the End Times. After all, it seemed as if Jesus meant Generation=Andrew, Peter, James, and John. In 95 AD, the last one standing is...John.

Yet sixty years earlier, when Peter understood Jesus wasn't being harsh but simply being forthright, he understood that he wasn't the one to get the job done. John was half his age (My theory...15). John is the youngest disciple, which gives him decades more life than Peter to get to places like Tahiti.

- So Peter asks about John.
- Jesus face-palms, knowing the Second Coming is 2,000 years later.
- Jesus sighs, knowing Peter is off-track
- Jesus tells Peter to focus on ministry since he's not going to live past 63 AD.
- Jesus makes an off-handed remark about John

Like most preachers, the scene focused on Peter, except for one little line:

**22 Jesus saith unto him, If I will that he tarry till I come, what is that to thee? follow thou me.**

Hold on? Tarry is a Shakespearean word meaning remain/wait. Did Jesus just get snarky with Peter? Jesus just referenced John remaining alive until the End Times, aka "I come." Peter interpreted "generation" to mean "the four of us." He was simply wondering how much time they, the four, had to get the job done. Jesus just made a HUGE promise:

- Spreading the Gospel to All Nations=not done by Peter.
- Spreading the Gospel to All Nations=not James or Andrew either.

- Spreading the Gospel to All Nations=John
- This Generation=not Peter
- This Generation=not James or Andrew either
- This Generation=John will witness the Seven Seals
- Has Jesus come back yet=No?
- Why? The Seven Seals haven't started the countdown.

And who will "tarry" until that time? John.

**If I will that he tarry till I come, what is that to thee?**

If this is all a bit complicated, imagine being John. For a bit, he might have been sitting there on the beach of Patmos, thinking to himself...YES, someone got to Tahiti. This is it! The End Times is now 1,335 Daniel Days away.

Then he started getting messages for the seven churches.

Dang, that'll add a few more months on. Maybe by my 80th birthday?

Then each seal is expanded upon, and all the symbolic meaning about the literal destruction of Jerusalem (preterist interpretations) goes global as each seal describes stuff that happens on a global scale. The details heard on the Mount of Olives are put into a timeline of sorts. For us, 2,000 years later, we barely understand how many seals we've seen, if any. Do I think the era of the White Horse was the missionary era ending with the evangelizing of Tahiti by the 20th century? Yep. Do I think the Red Horse was World War I, World War II, and the Cold War era that followed? Yep. Black Horse? Global inflation issues? Seems like it's happening? Or happened? Pale Horse? Oh, boy...is Covid a precursor? See, I can assume we're in the middle of the seals, but Seal 6 is UNDENIABLE. Nothing in the last 2,000 matches it.

And John?

He wrote it down with a shrug (I can't live past 120, right?)

Once he put a period in the final sentence of the Sixth Trumpet prophecy, he was probably expecting the next word to pertain to the Seventh Trumpet.

Nope.

He's told NOT to write.

**[Revelation 10:4] And when the seven thunders had uttered their voices, I was about to write: and I heard a voice from heaven saying unto me, Seal up those things which the seven thunders uttered, and write them not...(skipped verses) But in the days of the voice of the seventh angel, when he shall begin to sound, the mystery of God should be finished, as he hath declared to his servants the prophets.**

So John is given an oral message, which is supposed to be revealed in the "days" of the Seventh Angel. Whether that angel has a Seal, Trumpet, or Bowl, it means that it has not yet happened as I write this on January 16, 2022. But if John didn't write it down, how will we know what the message is?

**If I will that he tarry till I come, what is that to thee?**

Hold on. John was given a very special End Times message, and then was told not to share it with anyone until the time of the Seventh Angel. He can't share it if he's dead, right?

**If I will that he tarry till I come, what is that to thee?**

John knows his stuff. He knows he has sinned. He also knows that the penalty of sin is death, which is why he wanted to die as a martyr. Cool. Tarry? It had to have crossed his mind as his hair turned gray. When he grew more ear hair than scalp hair, **tarry** might have crossed his mind again. When he read the Ephesus Daily Bugle and learned of the last disciple dying as a martyr, he might have thought of **tarry**. As a ninety-year-old man, when the Romans knocked on his door and arrested him, he must have thought he was near the end of **tarry**. But when he shook himself off like a wet poodle next to Domitian's pot of oil, he knew **tarry** had come and gone again. Now, on Patmos, he is told to keep a secret message for the folks living during the time of the Seventh Angel. The words of Christ must have echoed in his mind:

**If I will that he tarry till I come, what is that to thee?**

"No, no, no, no, NO! I'm not going to live another 25 years." John might have a literal interpretation of the Genesis 6 line about "120 years." You see, some folks believe Noah was given a 120-year warning before the flood came. Others have interpreted the line to mean that humans would no longer live to the ripe old age of Methuselah (969 years). God changed things so that the average man lives a short life, and only special times, like Moses at 120, does anybody get to the maximum expiration date.

How can John preach the secret message?

**If I will that he tarry till I come, what is that to thee?**

It's almost impossible for a human to live past 120 years. Scoffers love to laugh at Genesis because we fall apart at 60, so how can we last to 600? Yes, you can hypothesize a different condition in the pre flood world to now, but com'on. It's not practical. It's impossible.

Oh wait.

John's angel is holding something.

## Maybe Manna?

In the pre-flood world of Genesis, God had not yet caused it to rain (very literal reading). It was only after the flood that modern day clouds appeared and the rainbow with it. Before the flood, the mist of God filled the earth each morning. It was this moisture that provided for all the needs of living creatures.

Hard to imagine, isn't it?

There was another aspect that was forever changed after the flood. Before the flood, living creatures could live on the "**herb of the earth**" that grew. After the flood, it was gone and Noah's family had to find a new food supply. Before the flood, this "**herb**" could sustain life indefinitely. What is exactly meant by "**herb**" of the earth? An herb is a delicate plant that can grow without much root structure because of high moisture. So Adam and Eve were vegetarians, and with plant life destroyed, they had to become carnivores? Not necessarily, seeds and plants survived the flood, yet this "**herb**" food was never eaten again.

Mist.

Sustaining food.

In the time of Moses, God led the Hebrews into the wilderness, a.k.a a big desert (probably Saudi Arabia, buy my other book!). Regardless of which desert, there was no food or water source able to sustain two million Hebrews. Impossible! But Moses records that:

**[Exodus 16:13]: and in the morning the dew lay round about the host. 14 And when the dew that lay was gone up, behold, upon the face of the wilderness there lay a small round thing, as small as the hoar frost on the ground. [15] And when the children of Israel saw it, they said one to another, It is manna: for they wist not what it was. And Moses said unto them, This is the bread which the LORD hath given you to eat.**

And later...

**[31] And the house of Israel called the name thereof Manna: and it was like coriander seed, white; and the taste of it was• like wafers made with honey. [32] And Moses said, This is the thing which the LORD commandeth, Fill an omer of it to be kept for your generations; that they may see the bread wherewith I have fed you in the wilderness, when I brought you forth from the land of Egypt. [33] And Moses said unto Aaron, Take a pot, and put an omer full of manna therein, and lay it up before the LORD, to be kept for your generations. [34] As the LORD commanded Moses, so Aaron laid it up before the Testimony, to be kept. [35] And the children of Israel did eat manna forty years, until they came to a land inhabited; they did eat manna, until they came unto the borders of the land of Canaan. [36] Now an omer is the tenth part of an ephah.**

For the next forty years, the Hebrews were sustained on this Manna. It was the perfect food. In fact, the book of Psalms calls Manna the **"Food of the Angels."** How do you feed and sustain two million in a desert? You give them Manna! Mist. Sustaining Food. Perhaps this seems like the same stuff from before the flood.

Elijah had another strange experience similar to these. He was being sent to go from Israel to Mt. Horeb, which is 40 days across a desert without food. To do so, I believe he also was given manna:

> **[1 Kings 19:5] And as he lay and slept under a juniper tree, behold, then an angel touched him, and said unto him, Arise and eat. [6] And he looked, and, behold, there was a cake baken on the coals, and a cruse of water at his head. And he did eat and drink, and laid him down again. [7 ]And the angel of the LORD came again the second time, and touched him, and said, Arise and eat; because the journey is too great for thee. [8] And he arose, and did eat and drink, and went in the strength of that meat forty days and forty nights unto Horeb the mount of God.**

Elijah eats the cake and it sustains him for the next 80+ days and he goes to and from Mt. Horeb. Before the flood, humans could live 900 years. How? Could it be manna? Angels are immortal creatures, yet there is "Angel Food." Why would they need to eat? Perhaps by eating manna, they are sustained. The Hebrews and Elijah needed to be sustained in a food-less/waterless environment…give 'em manna.

**If I will that he tarry till I come, what is that to thee?**

Jesus willed it that John remain until he returned. How does the Trinity make it happen? Give him manna! Look again at how John described the encounter:

> **[Revelation 10:8] And the voice which I heard from heaven spake unto me again, and said, Go and take the little book which is open in the hand of the angel which standeth upon the sea and upon the earth. [9] And I went unto the angel, and said unto him, Give me the little book. And he said unto me, Take it, and eat it up; and it shall make thy belly bitter, but it shall be in thy mouth sweet as honey. [10] And I took the little book**

**out of the angel's hand, and ate it up; and it was in my mouth sweet as honey: and as soon as I had eaten it, my belly was bitter. [11] And he said unto me, Thou must prophesy again before many peoples, and nations, and tongues, and kings.**

When the Hebrews ate manna, it tasted like honey. When Elijah ate manna, it looked like a little cake. When the Hebrews harvested manna, they prepared it like sheets of paper. John had never seen manna before. He described layers of a substance. Did he really eat a book? Take a bite of this book. Paper is not sweet!

**If I will that he tarry till I come, what is that to thee?**

The angel presented John this manna because Jesus willed John to remain. Manna could do it. Perhaps it was a double dose of manna. When John ate it, his stomach became bitter. Rotten manna? Hardly! John's stomach could have absorbed something that could sustain him for 2,000 years. Did Adam and Eve need digestive organs prior to the fall (why would you need to excrete waste product from a food that was perfect)? John ate the manna and his organs were rendered useless. Perhaps they just stopped or changed.

Without even considering the fact that John would need to be sustained for 2,000 years, how are the two living witnesses going to preach in Jerusalem? Will they need to take potty breaks? "Excuse me, enemies of God, I have to stop now so I can pee?" This manna was consumed by John to sustain him to death. His body was preserved. If Enoch lived before the flood, and the herb of the earth existed then, then could he be sustained as well?

The purpose for John eating this manna is clear (to me) from what the angel says to him next:

**"Thou must prophesy again."**

John asked for a good death—to die as a martyr—well, Jesus is about to explain how this promise will be delivered.

...in a big way.

# CHAPTER NINE

# A GOOD DEATH

So after John got done eating the book, and then measuring a virtual temple, he was all set. Set for what? A good death!

When the sons of Zebedee asked Jesus to be baptized the same way he was about to be baptized (martyr's death), John was ready to lead by example. He was ready to show folks that he could cast aside all the nets of materialism to live (and die) for the word of Christ.

Then a few years go by.

And then a few decades pass.

Opportunity after opportunity slipped through his fingers, until John found himself old and alone in Ephesus. If he thought Jesus had forgotten the promise, he only needed to wait until 95 A.D. before he understood what Jesus meant when he mentioned the need to tarry. As he wrote down the words that would become chapters 10 and 11 in the book of Revelation, it was probably happening pretty fast, and by the time the messengers moved on to the flashback chapters and then into all of the Antichrist stuff, he needed to just shake it off and keep writing to keep up.

Remember, he's essentially a secretary listening to the boss dictate. Christ (and John) finishes the book with another promise… **"I am coming quickly."**

The divine light diminishes…

And John is left sitting on the beach at Patmos.

If he was going to flip back through the stack of papers, I would bet he'd turn back to the part where he was given the sweet stuff and told to measure the temple.

Is he convinced yet he's one of the two witnesses?

Maybe (are you?).

The fact that the Book of Revelation ends with a promise of a quick return might indicate that he had not yet wrapped his mind around how long it'll be before Christ returns. Yet now he knows the manner and purpose of his death. Let's review what he would have gleaned.

## Prediction #1: All Nations

John has now been given two "End Times" accounts, beyond what he might have read in the Book of Enoch, which Peter and James the Just reference prior to what was given in Patmos. Sitting on the sands of Patmos, John begins to wrap his brain around the fact that Christ's promise that **"this generation"** now means only him, and that there is nothing on earth, including a pot of boiling oil, that can keep him from getting to the breaking of the Sixth Seal and his time in the temple.

Granted, he has no clue how many years it will take before the **"gospel is preached to all nations"** but he accepts the fact that he will **tarry** until the Sixth Seal is broken.

John didn't stay long on Patmos, which we will address in another chapter, so when he was released, it is obvious that he would have spread this prophecy to every church he knew, especially those seven churches addressed by Christ. His goal is to mobilize Christendom to get beyond the Mediterranean region and begin to get to places like Africa, Asia, and…(America? Australia? It was a bigger task than he imagined, huh?). Yet off he went…

## Prediction #2: The Temple

John grew up in Judea, and was a middle-aged man when General Titus besieged Jerusalem in the year 70 AD, and after an obstinate standoff, the city of Jerusalem was ravaged and the temple destroyed. If my theory about John's **tarry** is literal, then he did not die in the decades after receiving the secret message in Revelation 10:4. If so, then he also would have been around for the Bar Kobba revolt, when the whole of Judea was erased and a war of genocide led to the diaspora of the Jews. At this point, he must have realized it would be quite a while before two witnesses could preach in a rebuilt temple.

And still we wait.

There are many Christian scholars who believe a rebuilding of the temple will be a trigger for the End Times to begin, so let's look at what was told to John:

**[Revelation 11: 1] And there was given me a reed like unto a rod: and the angel stood, saying, Rise, and measure the temple**

**of God, and the altar, and them that worship therein. [2] But the court which is without the temple leave out, and measure it not; for it is given unto the Gentiles: and the holy city shall they tread under foot forty and two months. [3] And I will give power unto my two witnesses, and they shall prophesy a thousand two hundred and threescore days, clothed in sackcloth. [4] These are the two olive trees, and the two candlesticks standing before the God of the earth.**

Okay, so John is certainly given a rod to measure. I've speculated that when Ezekiel and Zachariah witnessed "the dude" measuring the temple, they passed the measurements to the builders of Temple 2.0. If John is "the dude" with the measurements of the temple, then yes, it is totally possible for him to serve as the architect for the rebuilding of Temple 3.0.

Currently, there is a great deal of hatred and animosity between Christian/Jew and Muslims. Although we're all from the Abraham family tree of God-folks, the past two thousand years have made us enemies (Exhibit A: the Crusades). Our biggest obstacle? Islam has claimed the foundation of the old temple and put a Mosque on it. For a new Temple to be built, we'd need to knock down a holy shrine to Islam, starting World War III.

Or so it would seem.

What's up with this verse? **But the court which is without the temple leave out, and measure it not; for it is given unto the Gentiles:**

John the tape-measurer is told to get the dimensions, but then is told that there is a section that he's supposed to "leave out." How do you rebuild something while leaving out the measurements?

What is the purpose of the measuring?

Look at what the witnesses do. They are told to specifically measure the place known as the Holiest of Holies, where the Ark of the Covenant once rested. They are also told to measure the temple building itself. From within this area, the two witnesses will stand.

So I think it is possible that if Seals #6 and #7 cracked today, John and (Enoch) could walk up to the foundations of Temple 2.0, and standing within the space where the walls once stood, begin their **one thousand two hundred and threescore days** of witnessing. Would it annoy the Muslims whose Temple is nearby? Yep. Night and day, the two witnesses would remind Muslims, Atheists, etcetera (Mormons?), etcetera (Catholics?), etcetera (Protestants) of the truest message of Christ (Guess we'll find out which denomination is right on that day, huh?). The truth will be boldly declared for all to hear, whether we'll want to listen or not.

So, no, the walls do not need to stand for this to happen.

John knows where he can stand.

## Prediction #3: Sorcerer Battle

If you've read/heard my Examining Moses series, you might understand how the Priests of Belial, Jannes and Jambres, went toe to toe with the miracles of Moses and Aaron for the first few plagues.

It was a pretty epic "wizard" battle.

In the same way, the Two Witnesses will go toe-to-toe with the forces of evil.

**[Revelation 11:5] And if any man will hurt them, fire proceedeth out of their mouth, and devoureth their enemies: and if any man will hurt them, he must in this manner be killed. [6] These have power to shut heaven, that it rain not in the days of their prophecy: and have power over waters to turn them to blood, and to smite the earth with all plagues, as often as they will.**

Fire from their mouth? Drought? Blood water? Anything you can do, I can undo better? Wow, John is about to be bestowed with some pretty gnarly wizard skills, huh?

But wait…

Remember when the Beloved Disciple got dressed down by Jesus?

**[Luke 9:51]: As the day of His ascension approached, Jesus resolutely set out for Jerusalem. 52 He sent messengers on ahead, who went into a village of the Samaritans to make arrangements for Him. 53 But the people there refused to welcome Him, because He was heading for Jerusalem. 54 When the disciples James and John saw this, they asked, "Lord, do You want us to call down fire from heaven to consume them?" 55 But Jesus turned and rebuked them. 56 And He and His disciples went on to another village.**

Weird detail: What led John to believe he COULD do this?

Yes, you read correctly, John heard of Samaritans dissing Jesus and asked permission to destroy the village with fire from the sky. Holy Heck, Batman!

Of course, Jesus rebuked them. He wants converts. He wants folks to repent. He does not want sizzled Samaritans. Preach the Gospel to all nations, John! Don't be a Jonah!

Yet somewhere in an unwritten moment with Jesus, John and James believed they could do such a thing. Honestly, I think Jesus had a private moment with John (near James) where he pre-previewed his abilities as one of the Two Witnesses. Why the sneak peak? So John could learn humility to learn this power should only be used on those during the End Times (apparently this point was lost on the folks during the Reformation era).

## Prediction #4: Their Enemies

The Beloved Disciple, the Son of Thunder, was a spiritual heavyweight from an early age. He was trained by Mickey Goldmill, Duke Evers, and Apollo Creed (John the Baptist and Mary) for a major fight. His opponent?

**[Revelation 11:7] And when they shall have finished their testimony, the beast that ascendeth out of the bottomless pit shall make war against them, and shall overcome them, and kill them.**

The Beast from the Bottomless Pit?

There are a few beasts mentioned in the Book of Revelation (along with Beasts from Daniel), so I'll do my best to explain them all here:

Rev 12: The Red "water" Dragon (also the Leviathan=Satan

Rev 13: Beast from the Sea=the Antichrist dude, with symbolic reference to Satan.

Rev 13: Beast from the Earth=the Antichrist's powerful prophet (Judas bloodline).

Rev 9: Beast from the Bottomless Pit=Apollyon

Who?

So to be clear, John is not battling Team Antichrist or Satan himself, but instead, the Demon King, Apollyon. The two names given, Apollyon and Abaddon, both translate to "The Destroyer," which is a pretty kick-butt name.

In this corner, the Son of Thunder.

Wearing black trunks, the Destroyer from Down Under!

The identity of this dark figure varies from Belial, Perdition incarnate, to just some sinister angel locked up long ago (Azazel from Book of Enoch). Regardless of WHO John gets to fight, he knows going into it that he will lose. But look at the language—it describes how the Two Witnesses make **war** against Apollyon and his demon horde. War! He doesn't just get arrested, sentenced, and beheaded—John gets to go out in a supernatural cloud of chaos.

And guess what?

There is no sighting of Apollyon after this verse!

While there are specific "deaths" for the Antichrist, his Prophet, Satan, Death, and Hades, there is not a mention of Apollyon getting it. Does this mean it is a Ragnarok-esque Death-Draw! How Viking is that? John and (Enoch) die, but they take out one of the all-time fiends.

Hey Jesus, can I die a martyr's death?

Sure, John, how about dying in a death-draw with Apollyon?

Sign me up!

So, no, the walls do not need to stand for this to happen.

John knows where he can stand.

# Prediction #5: A Similar Death

Let's take a look at that promise made long ago, when John asked Jesus not just for a special place in Heaven but to die in a similar manner.

**[Mark 10:32] And they were in the way going up to Jerusalem; and Jesus went before them: and they were amazed; and as they followed, they were afraid. And he took again the twelve, and began to tell them what things should happen unto him, [33] Saying, Behold, we go up to Jerusalem; and the Son of man shall be delivered unto the chief priests, and unto the scribes; and they shall condemn him to death, and shall deliver him to the Gentiles: [34] And they shall mock him, and shall scourge him, and shall spit upon him, and shall kill him: and the third day he shall rise again.[35] And James and John, the sons of Zebedee, come unto him, saying, Master, we would that thou shouldest do for us whatsoever we shall desire. [36] And he said unto them, What would ye that I should do for you? [37] They said unto him, Grant unto us that we may sit, one on thy right hand, and the other on thy left hand, in thy glory. [38] But Jesus said unto them, Ye know not what ye ask: can ye drink of the cup that I drink of? and be baptized with the baptism that I am baptized with? [39] And they said unto him, We can. And Jesus said unto them, Ye shall indeed drink of the cup that I drink of; and with the baptism that I am baptized withal shall ye be baptized: [40] But to sit on my right hand and on my left hand is not mine to give; but it shall be given to them for whom it is prepared.**

Even though Jesus clarified that he'd only grant such a death to one of "whom it is prepared," he agrees and says to them that they'd metaphorically be baptized with the blood of martyrdom. For James, it was a beheading. For John, it is as follows:

**[Revelation 11:8] And their dead bodies shall lie in the street of the great city, which spiritually is called Sodom and Egypt, where also our Lord was crucified. [9] And they of the people and kindreds and tongues and nations shall see their dead bodies three days and an half, and shall not suffer their dead bodies to be put in graves. [10] And they that dwell upon the earth shall rejoice over them, and make merry, and shall send gifts one to another; because these two prophets tormented them that dwelt on the earth.**

**[11] And after three days and an half the Spirit of life from God entered into them, and they stood upon their feet; and great fear fell upon them which saw them. [12] And they heard a great voice from heaven saying unto them, Come up hither. And they ascended up to heaven in a cloud; and their enemies beheld them. [13] And the same hour was there a great earthquake, and the tenth part of the city fell, and in the earthquake were slain of men seven thousand: and the remnant were affrighted, and gave glory to the God of heaven.**

So not only does John get to be a martyr (like Jesus), but he gets to get killed in Jerusalem (like Jesus), have his corpse displayed publicly (like Jesus), and come back to life after three days (like Jesus), but then cause the spiritually neutral to give glory as the final crop of Christians to be saved.

But hey, if you want to believe Victorinus, and think John died of old age in Ephesus, go right ahead.

But then your Jesus lied to John about his "baptism."

My Jesus is going to give him an epic death, worthy of the Beloved Disciple.

Which leads to the question...where's John been all this while?

# CHAPTER TEN

# THE WANDERING JEW

Whatcha talkin' 'bout, Willis?

If it's a difficult pill to swallow (John as the witness), why is it easier to accept that Jesus was crucified, poked with a spear, put in the ground for three days, and then...presto! If God can allow the rules of our world to be suspended for the Christ, why can't the Christ suspend the rules of our world for a witness?

It's an interesting line of thought to walk in John's shoes in the days that followed the encounter on Patmos.

It does seem as if he was physically changed, since he discussed how it tasted and felt in his stomach. My theory holds that he ate something akin to Manna, which for the Hebrews, Elijah(?), and the antediluvian patriarchs (?) meant sustained or extended lives. What if the death clock just stopped ticking for John? He's just "pickled" his body, preserving it at the age of seventy-five (ish) for the next few thousand years?

Wow, the creative possibilities are unlimited.

Did John get a flaming chariot like Elijah and was whisked away to Heaven, undead, for another overly complicated death at a future date in time?

Did he just vanish like Enoch, when God "took him" and he was found "no more"?

Or did he walk the earth like that guy from Kung Fu?

Interestingly enough, there are some strange tales that came out of this era.

## The Reason for the Rumor

One of them is mentioned by John himself. Remember the Tarry scene?

**[John 21:20] Then Peter, turning about, seeth the disciple whom Jesus loved following; which also leaned on his breast at supper, and said, Lord, which is he that betrayeth thee? 21 Peter seeing him saith to Jesus, Lord, and what shall this man do? [22] Jesus saith unto him, If I will that he tarry till I come, what is that to thee? follow thou me. [23] Then went this saying abroad among the brethren, that that disciple should not die: yet Jesus said not unto him, He shall not die; but, If I will that he tarry till I come, what is that to thee?**
**[24] This is the disciple which testifieth of these things, and wrote these things: and we know that his testimony is true.**
**[25] And there are also many other things which Jesus did, the which, if they should be written every one, I suppose that even the world itself could not contain the books that should be written. Amen.**

A saying abroad among the brethren? In other words, a rumor. Folks began to whisper that John was an immortal, that John had been changed during his time in the oil pot or on Patmos. John mentioned the rumor in the sentence after he brought up Christ's promise that he'd **tarry.** Folks either interpreted the line correctly OR they saw with their own eyes that John no longer aged. Regardless, John clarified that he wasn't an immortal (since he knew he'd die as a witness i.e. martyr) but that he could in fact die (be killed). John then brings up that he has secret knowledge not written down (remember that moment in Rev 11?). But where is the proof that John references? He said **"we know that his testimony is true"** by referencing the **tarry** conversation.

Converts want miracles, right? Instead, we've had to have faith since the days of Christ, right? But here, John says the folks who know him know it's true. Is he suggesting that he is Exhibit A on why we should believe everything else written down? We'll get back to that in Chapter 12.

Along with John's own "rumor" reference, there is another HUGE bit of mythology that came from this time period. Sitting on my bookshelf is The Legend of the Wandering Jew by George K. Anderson, who is even nerdier than me! His 500 page textbook is a thorough research text about this tale. What's the tale? There are dozens and dozens of tales about a nomadic Jewish man who wanders in and out of European villages.

During the Medieval Era, it was a well known tale with four hundred pages of variations. Mr. Anderson tries to understand the origins of the legend, and while he also mentions Biblical accounts of Malchus, as either the one-eared soldier or the cheek striker; and Ahasuerues, as a really old origin for one cursed with unnatural life by God; he also identifies the origin of the legend with John.

A 13th Century John sighting? While the Dark Ages might have been a good time for John to come out of hiding, Anderson points out that most legends about John do NOT have him dying of old age in Ephesus. There is a lot of odd lore and legends which have John hanging around for much longer, which is explained by simply having other Christians named John, right? Having grown up with Michael Landon's Highway to Heaven series, I like this romanticized idea of the Real Deal, John the Beloved Disciple, going from village to village, preaching the Gospel as an unidentified Wandering Jew. When travel and communication improved, it's no wonder the tale gained traction in the 13th century...Hey! We have a Wandering Jew story in our town, also!

## A Tall Tale

While the Legend of the Wandering Jew is a bit fanciful, there is actually a tale recorded by Eusebius (via Clement) about John. Here's what was written:

**"Listen to a tale, which is not a mere tale, but a narrative concerning John the apostle, which has been handed down and treasured up in memory. For when, after the tyrant's death, he returned from the isle of Patmos to Ephesus, he went away upon their invitation to the neighboring territories of the Gentiles, to appoint bishops in some places, in other places to set in order whole churches, elsewhere to choose to the ministry some one of those that were pointed out by the Spirit.**

When he had come to one of the cities not far away, and had consoled the brethren in other matters, he finally turned to the bishop that had been appointed, and seeing a youth of powerful physique, of pleasing appearance, and of ardent temperament, he said, 'This one I commit to thee in all earnestness in the presence of the Church and with Christ as witness.'

And when the bishop had accepted the charge and had promised all, he repeated the same injunction with an appeal to the same witnesses, and then departed for Ephesus.

But the presbyter, taking home the youth committed to him, reared, kept, cherished, and finally baptized him. After this he relaxed his stricter care and watchfulness, with the idea that in putting upon him the seal of the Lord he had given him a perfect protection.

But some youths of his own age, idle and dissolute, and accustomed to evil practices, corrupted him when he was thus prematurely freed from restraint. At first they enticed him by costly entertainments; then, when they went forth at night for robbery, they took him with them, and finally they demanded that he should unite with them in some greater crime. He gradually became accustomed to such practices, and on account of the positiveness of his character, leaving the right path, and taking the bit in his teeth like a hard-mouthed and powerful horse, he rushed the more violently down into the depths. And finally despairing of salvation in God, he no longer meditated what was insignificant, but having committed some great crime, since he was now lost once for all, he expected to suffer a like fate with the rest. Taking them, therefore, and forming a band of robbers, he became a bold bandit-chief, the most violent, most bloody, most cruel of them all.

Time passed, and some necessity having arisen, they sent for John. But he, when he had set in order the other matters on account of which he had come, said,'Come, O bishop, restore us the deposit which both I and Christ committed to thee, the church, over which thou presidest, being witness."

But the bishop was at first confounded, thinking that he was falsely charged in regard to money which he had not received, and he could neither believe the accusation respecting what he had not, nor could he disbelieve John.

But when he said, 'I demand the young man and the soul of the brother,' the old man, groaning deeply and at the same time bursting into tears, said, 'He is dead.'

'How and what kind of death?'

'He is dead to God,' he said; 'for he turned wicked and abandoned, and at last a robber. And now, instead of the church, he haunts the mountain with a band like himself.'

But the Apostle rent his clothes, and beating his head with great lamentation, he said, 'A fine guard I left for a brother's soul! But let a horse be brought me, and let some one show me the way.'

He rode away from the church just as he was, and coming to the place, he was taken prisoner by the robbers' outpost. He, however, neither fled nor made entreaty, but cried out, 'For this did I come; lead me to your captain.'

The latter, meanwhile, was waiting, armed as he was. But when he recognized John approaching, he turned in shame to flee.

But John, forgetting his age, pursued him with all his might, crying out, 'Why, my son, dost thou flee from me, thine own father, unarmed, aged? Pity me, my son; fear not; thou hast still hope of life. I will give account to Christ for thee. If need be, I will willingly endure thy death as the Lord suffered death for us. For thee will I give up my life. Stand, believe; Christ hath sent me.'

And he, when he heard, first stopped and looked down; then he threw away his arms, and then trembled and wept bitterly. And when the old man approached, he embraced him, making confession with lamentations as he! Was able, baptizing himself a second time with tears, and concealing only his right hand, But John, pledging himself, and assuring him on oath that he would find forgiveness with the Saviour, besought him, fell upon his knees, kissed his right hand itself as if now purified by repentance, and led him back to the church.

**And making intercession for him with copious prayers, and struggling together with him in continual fastings, and subduing his mind by various utterances, he did not depart, as they say, until he had restored him to the church, furnishing a great example of true repentance and a great proof of regeneration, a trophy of a visible resurrection."**

Quite a story, huh? And it certainly could just be a tale, but the great researcher, Eusebius, saw fit to include it in his chronicling of the Christian Church.

First, notice how Clement's story puts the time as AFTER John's exile on Patmos. Again, my theory has John at a minimum of 75 years old, but this is the youngest he'd be, isn't it? The guy who just received the Revelation of Christ would have been motivated! What does Clement say he did? He went on a regional tour, visiting...yep, the Seven Churches and also to the territory of the Gentiles. It appears as if John, at the age of 75, is going to try to spread the gospel to all nations himself.

Next, notice how John also understands that he needs to recruit the next generation to carry the torch. What kind of disciple does he choose? One that is robust! Why? Think about it...John knows the gospel needs to be spread to all nations. That's on him. He's the "delay" in keeping Christ from coming back. It's on him to get things organized on earth. While history records the "Church of Peter" evangelizing the heathen nations (with a sword), at the time, the "Churches of Paul" were far stronger, which is where John went to mobilize. After an untold time (at least a few more years), John visits a nearby city/church, and identifies our nameless Robber King as the right stuff for future ministries.

Now, the theme of this lesson is impressive. In it, it clarifies that a baptism won't give you immunity from future sin. That dude went dark, didn't he? In a way, it describes how the brighter the light you have, the harder evil works on you. The dude knew better, and when he fell, his own guilt for his sin darkened his ways.

Then John becomes a walking metaphor for the love of Christ. Did John just give up on him because he was obviously evil? Nope. You are mine! What an awesome lesson in Christianity 101.

## Time to Tarry

But let's get back to the "**Tarry Theory.**" This story takes a young man and leaves off with a man who's the leader of a criminal enterprise. This plot takes place over a decade or more. With the church tour and the education and depredation of the dude, I think we could safely tack +15 years onto the age of John by the end of the story, meaning he's 90ish now. Does he act 90?

NO! He hops on a horse like he's Legolas, then he fearlessly rides into the mountain strong hold of a bunch of murders, and then when seeing the dude, he RUNS HIM DOWN! To be the Robber King, you have to be the Blackbeard of the pirates. You have to make them fear you, right? But John causes this guy to wet the bed and run.

Now, I certainly like the idea of the man's guilt causing him to run. Yes, that really works, but think about this also...the Robber King is years older, but John...he hasn't aged a day!

That could be what freaks him out, right? Also, if he spent any time with John, he knows this was a man who was boiled in oil and survived. And from the look on his face, he's not happy.

I'd like to remind the readers of a funny anecdote written by John himself. While Mathew, Mark, and Luke all give us bits and pieces of the Easter Scene, John also adds his POV from that morning. Remember how Luke (via Peter) wrote **"Then arose Peter, and ran into the sepulchre"** (Luke 24:12). When John read this, he wrote his own account in 20:4 **"So they both ran together, and the other disciple did out-run Peter, and came FIRST to the sepulchre."** How funny is John?! He made sure that everyone knew he was faster than Peter, but...age before beauty. I bring this funny nugget up because 90+ years after his birth, John runs down a barbarian who is still in his prime!

How is this possible?

Do you remember how Moses was 120 years old but still looked good? Those "manna eaters" lived on no other source of nutrition than manna. Remember how angels ministered to Jesus and restored his health? How Eljiah walked out into the "wilderness" to hang out at Mount Horeb? This is why I think John's wafer stuff he was given restored his body and also preserved it. Remember Jack LaLande and Regis Philbin at 75? No? How about Sly Stallone and Arnold? Ah, that's a fit 75, isn't it? He's old, but he's a healthy old.

The most shocking thing found in this tale is what John said to the Robber King. Remember, John asked Jesus decades earlier to die a martyr's death, and for sixty years, he was denied that request. Then, on Patmos, he's given the BIG NEWS! He's now promised to be one of the two witnesses, destined to die within the blueprint foundation of the Temple, going toe-to-toe with major forces of evil. Epic!

Now, he's willing to throw all that away just to redeem the soul of one guy. He'd trade his life for the worthless life of the Robber King. Except he doesn't see sinners as worthless, does he? John no longer wants to drop fire on a village of Samaritans. He wants to save even the most worthless members of society.

John gets it.

Now...what to do with that knowledge?

# CHAPTER ELEVEN

# THE "FAKE NEWS" FIGHTER

In Greek language, which was the chosen language to write during this era (Thanks, Alexander), the word for knowledge is gnosi. Knowledge sounds like a wonderful thing, doesn't it. We've created a public education system and college to promote knowledge. It's an attribute, right? Who would argue that knowledge is bad. After all, the word Gospel is simply 'good news.' Knowledge is power! Jesus is the WORD, and words bring knowledge.

However...something very strange developed during the first century. While the Jews and Romans tried to simply stomp out the fire of Christianity, a much more diabolical plan developed, thwarting the growth of Christianity...Fake News.

Today, with an unregulated media mess where anybody can be a journalist without training or vetting by an independent editorial system, the algorithm-selected news popping up on our phones gives only perspectives on truth. It's deceitful chaos, isn't it? In the time of John, something similar happened to Christianity, and in an Orwellian twist of logic, the perpetrators of the BIG LIE would be called...Gnostics.

The practice was quite simple: steal the identity of Christianity.

What does that mean? As the real Christians like Peter, Thomas, Barnabas, Mary Magdalene, James, Phillip, and John spread the 'good news," the concepts of Christianity began to take root and the early disciples became Christian folk heroes. The people who converted to Christianity in these days walked the walk, and the martyrs only fanned the flames of this growing religion of do-gooders. Instead of trying to stomp out Christianity, the Gnostics simply muddied the waters, ruining the good name and message. They stole the name of someone like James but changed the message to one very different than the message of Christ.

I've spent WAY too much time going down this rabbit hole, and trust me, it leads to some very dark stuff. If Christianity was the religion of the LIGHT, then Gnosticism seems to be the religion of the DARKNESS. Some believe it was hatched by Simon the Magus (the guy from Acts), but others feel it existed long before the first century, and like a parasite, it simply finds a new host and new set of names to spread its dark humanist philosophy.

Most historians, though, strongly believe that Gnosticism didn't blossom until the Second Century, which is supported by history and archeology, including recent discovery of many texts that predate the oldest physical copies of our New Testament (we have copies of copies, but NOT third century inventions, as our detractors say). By the time the Romans helped create the Roman Catholic Church, and effectively weed out all the Gnostic filth, the red drop of deceit into a clear pool had diluted the message for the unconverted. It was quite a mess to sort out. Who said what? What does Christianity mean?

For this reason, in the third century, Emperor Constantine asked for the Council of Nicaea to make a simple creed, and after this, the message became "orthodox" or Catholic. Beginning with Eusebius and culminating with St. Jerome's unofficially official canon of Biblical texts, Christianity had to sort through these Gnostic texts circulating.

But when Gnosticism rose to power in the second century, Christianity was vulnerable. If somebody from a nearby Church had a letter from James...how did you know if it was safe or poison? Who could sort things out for you?

(has anybody seen John?)

## Who wrote what?

So you now understand how the Gnostics made folks question facts, including authorship. Today, we can analyze the language of these received texts, which were translated into Latin from the original Greek and Hebrew. Careers can be made on proper understanding of Greek verbs, right scholars? Both scoffers and Gnostics want you to have as much doubt about the inspiration and credibility of the Biblical texts.

Because of this, many Bible commentators have gone on record with the belief that there are three Johns: one who wrote the Gospel, one who wrote the letters, and one who wrote Revelation. The reason these claims are made is based on some solid scholarship about writing style and contextual reference. I can't ignore these claims. After all, there is a distinct difference between the way "John" references himself, how he writes, etc.

Plus, how could he write against Gnosticism in the second century, when you know…(too old to be alive)?

Even though my theory is the most preposterous, it makes things work. It keeps a tight narrative, also. So obviously, John wrote the Revelation immediately, giving copies to the seven churches and then some. This was his first written work.

Then, the days, weeks, months, years begin to tick off…

He remains "frozen in time" at the age of 75, getting older but not aging (like Moses). Decades go by, the Penitent Thief anecdote happens, and suddenly, we're smack dab in the middle of the second century with Gnostics on the run!

## First, First John

So I'm going to touch on some of the cool things that I've noticed in John, but I'll mostly be sticking to the verses that support the theory that (1+1+1=1 John). In other words, support for John being alive during the course of all three texts.

- 1:1-5: He uses the Christ=Light=Word like the Gospel
- 2:1: He uses "My little children" or "Beloved" to show that he's an older, fatherly figure decades beyond his audience.
- 2:18: He writes about the "Antichrist is coming, even now many antichrists have come," which seems to reflect

the idea given in Revelation that (5 have been, 1 is, 1 will be, and 5+1+1=8th).

**[3:8]: "For this purpose the Son of God was manifested, that he might destroy the works of the devil."**

- In other words, God and Satan are not gnostic polar opposites. Having written Revelation, he understands that Christ's purpose is to fix us and deal with Satan.

**[4:3] And every spirit that confesseth not that Jesus Christ is come in the flesh is not of God: and this is that spirit of antichrist, whereof ye have heard that it should come; and even now already is it in the world.**

- This is the "proof" that scholars use to deny John as the Apostle. This is the root of Gnosticism, which tries to redefine Christ as not even being a human. See the problem? John connects the philosophy of Gnosticism with the Antichrist (which is bad).

**[5:16] If any man see his brother sin a sin which is not unto death, he shall ask, and he shall give him life for them that sin not unto death. There is a sin unto death: I do not say that he shall pray for it. [17] All unrighteousness is sin: and there is a sin not unto death.**

- Again, this is addressing the Gnostic "anything goes" philosophy, which seems much more dire.
- And then he finishes with a passage on rejecting "fake good news."

# Second John

Just the salutations on this one garner fascination. He starts off the letter with the enigmatic "The Elder." Again, with a conservative theory, John outlasts the other disciples by decades, so no one is "elder" to him. He's claiming his new identity, and seems to be using his stamp of approval to make his letter legit.

**[1:1] to the elect lady and her children, whom I love in the truth; and not I only, but also all they that have known the truth.**

- Again, context matters, otherwise you could have this be a fruitful Virgin Mary (not), Mary Magdalene (not), or some other unknown woman. Yet in the context of the second century, who could **she** be? The possibilities are endless, but consider this: the Church. Remember Revelation 12? The woman? 12 stars? While I feel this is a flashback to the Holy Spirit (does gender matter?), it could also be a symbolic representation of the Holy Spirit within the church. What is the Holy Spirit if not that what dwells within us? This would be a poetic address to folks who've read his Revelation.

**[1:7] For many deceivers are entered into the world, who confess not that Jesus Christ is come in the flesh. This is a deceiver and an antichrist. [8] Look to yourselves, that we lose not those things which we have wrought, but that we receive a full reward.**

- Again, John seems to be directly addressing the Gnostic threat of the Second Century. The Gnostics viewed flesh as evil and an abomination to the true God. To them, the BAD GOD is the one who made the material universe. The GOOD GOD (Satan/Belial) is disgusted by flesh, which is why they felt Jesus as a human was an abomination. John reminds his followers that the WHOLE POINT of Jesus coming in flesh is to prove Satan was wrong. John clarifies that Gnostics are the bad guys by connecting them to Team Antichrist.

## Third John

These letters keep getting shorter, don't they? But the reason the early Christians kept them is that they were the shield against a powerful spiritual attack from the lying Gnostics. The Gnostics tried to ruin the infant Christendom by confusing the population about what it stood for. To this date, the History Channel and others will muddy the waters around holidays by talking about "lost" Gospels the Church didn't want you know about.

This is what John dealt with in his letters.

John helped his "children" weather a story caused by false teachers. Christ's plan for John seems pretty obvious now, doesn't it? By leaving one disciple to **tarry** until he returns, John was able to say "nuh uh" to any charismatic false teacher.

**[3:9] I wrote unto the church: but Diotrephes, who loveth to have the preeminence among them, receiveth us not. [10] Wherefore, if I come, I will remember his deeds which he doeth, prating against us with malicious words: and not content therewith, neither doth he himself receive the brethren, and forbiddeth them that would, and casteth them out of the church. [11] Beloved, follow not that which is evil,**

**but that which is good. He that doeth good is of God: but he that doeth evil hath not seen God. [12] Demetrius hath good report of all men, and of the truth itself: yea, and we also bear record; and ye know that our record is true.**

- I'd hate to be Demetrius the day THE JOHN shows up to set the record straight. Yes, he's a popular celebrity, but look at his works! His works were evil.
- You can see him "weaning" the early church away from his "seal of approval" with a pretty obvious philosophy.
- But he finishes with the stamp of approval that HE, the Elder, has "seen" Jesus, which makes his record true.

How is this not the same John? John did not want to become Pope John, nor did he want to tackle evil himself. Like Christ, he simply wanted to teach the early Church how to stay on the path. Eusebius (28.4) collected another anecdote about John via Irenaeus via Polycarp (I know, it's like citing Wikipedia):

**"One day John the apostle went into a bath-house to take a bath, but when he found out that Cerinthus was inside he leapt from the spot and ran for the door, as he could not endure to be under the same roof. He urged his companions to do the same, calling out: 'Let us get out of here, for fear the place falls in, now that Cerinthus, the enemy of truth, is inside.'"**

The takeaways from this anecdote? Cerinthus was a Gnostic preacher, who undermined the message of New Jerusalem with his own version, given to him by angels, also, about how sexual orgies will lead you to a quality understanding of God. Lies. Again, evil propaganda spread to counter the distribution of Revelation. Like the angel Michael, John is not about to debate evil, for he knows the danger of debating lies. Instead, he models isolating himself from the lure of evil. He alludes to his companions that God, not him, will deal with the likes of Cerinthus.

It makes me wonder if John didn't just isolate himself from the lure of evil and the taint of wicked men. Remember how Jesus would take off for quiet spots? I'm beginning to think John might have gone to the mountains, and instead of a chariot to Heaven, he's just hanging out like some monk. He might even have a YouTube Channel. Who knows?

I do know that before he went "off the grid," he had one more important message for the "little children" in his flock.

# CHAPTER TWELVE

# THE GOSPEL OF JOHN

Believing John lived long enough to deal with the Gnostics is not too outlandish, but anything longer than a Moses or Abraham lifespan (which would be modern miracles) invites a bit of eye-rolling and disbelief. After all, we have records of John's death...

Our legendary researcher, Eusebius, includes a "death of John" anecdote in his famous work. In it, he writes:

**"In Asia, great luminaries sleep who shall rise again on the last day, the day of the Lord's advent, when He is coming with glory from Heaven and shall search out all of His saints...**

**Again there is John, who leant back on the Lord's breast, and became a priest wearing the mitre, a martyr and teacher; he too sleeps in Ephesus."**

So there!

Fact!

As much as I'd like to argue that "sleep" does not mean "death," it seems pretty obvious what the writer, Polycrates, meant in his letter to Victor, Bishop of Rome. Asia is Turkey, and Ephesus is Ephesus, so this letter that found its way into the hands of the Roman Catholic Church, who followed John's lead about getting an orthodox message to fight against the Gnostics, is our undeniable bit of evidence.

But when did John become a priest?

And when did he die as a martyr? I thought the rest of tradition spoke of him dying of old age?

And who is this Polycrates guy?

Oh, the "Bishop of Rome" Victor tried to cut him off for some of his views the rest of Christendom deemed heretical, yet the letter remained, didn't it? It's easier to believe in reason (or a lie) than to trust a miracle, right?

John was buried in Ephesus.

Polycrates said so.

Accept this one account...and ignore a whole lot of other inexplicable moments.

I couldn't do it, so when my wife the travel agent started throwing out ideas for a vacation, I was like...please, please, PLEASE, can we do that cruise from the brochure.

The cruise was pretty commercial, but it let me visit all the important stops. We began in Rome, and then sailed to the Island of Patmos, where I had two choices for excursions: the Cave of John or...hanging out on the beach.

Being a big dope, I went to the cave, where John supposedly served his sentence. It had all sorts of goofy variant tales about his time on Patmos, but most didn't match scripture or even match reason. Once I finished, I realized I should have gone down to the beach, which is where John had to be when the angel stood with one foot on the shore and one on the water.

Duh!

What a mistake.

They loaded us on the ship, and ultimately, I got to disembark at the ancient city of Ephesus. I traveled up into the mountains where I visited the foundation of a house that is believed to be the one where John brought Mary. It gave me goose bumps and felt perfectly legit (even if it'd been turned into a tourist stop.).

The crowning moment of the trip, however, is when I got to visit a church dedicated to St. John. As the tour guide explained, it was not a first or second century church, but one built much later. Ok. Then he took us on a tour of paintings and old school architecture before finishing at…the place where John's bones were kept.

Really? The bones belonging to the Son of Thunder?

We gathered around in a big circle while our guide told us about the lore surrounding it. There was a strange grate above an underground chasm, which is where a small underground stream flowed. Yep, folks had to be kept from drinking this miracle juice, which explained the grate. Then the guide explained that early lore spoke about the bones rattling about in the tomb.

Okay, okay, okay…

I had to raise my hand.

If the church itself was not built until centuries after the "era" of John, then where did the bones come from? If there was no ceremony, funeral, and placing the bones into the prepared tomb, then the bones had to be buried somewhere prior, right? Where did they find the bones? At this, the guide referenced that they transferred the bones from a location out in the hills to the new church.

Hmm...

So there I stood, over a set of bones, asking God to reconcile what our guide and Polycrates claimed and to reconcile this with the promises that Christ made to John.

You will be baptized with the same baptism...

This generation shall not pass away...

The Gospel preached to all nations...

You shall testify again...

If I will it that he tarries 'til I come again...

Hello, man in the box, any counter arguments? Otherwise, I'm going with the words of Jesus rather than my guide and a dude named Polycrates.

I walked away, resolved.

John is awesome enough without being one of the two witnesses, but you chose me to throw some "out of the box" theories at you, right?

## The Rylands Papyrus

Long before the internet and apps like Biblehub.com made research SO MUCH EASIER, I had a collection of a dozen Bibles with different translations and even from different centuries. I loved to compare how things were worded in English. Some were straight scripture and others had commentary, introductions, and all that good stuff found as footnotes at the bottom. While I respect anybody who's risen to a prominent place in evaluating scripture for the publishing houses to make money with a "new and improved" edition, these writers are not infallible, are they? Heck, they don't even agree with each other, do they? If they agreed, we'd be back to old Orthodox Catholicism, yet even Catholic scholars couldn't stay on the same page (thanks, Luther).

In my hands, I held a New King James version, which appeared to be put together by mostly Baptist scholars. Okay, let's keep an open mind. The editor of this Bible, Earl D. Radmacher, had a pretty informative edition, which quickly became one of my favorites (which explains the duct tape holding it together to this date). Now, like all scholars, I had some things I agreed with and others I'd roll my eyes at. But I liked it.

So when I was building my list of arguments about John as the Witness, I found some strange things written in the introduction to the Gospel of John. In it, Earl writes:

**"In the nineteenth century, many critics claimed that the Gospel of John was written around A.D. 170. Then in 1935, C.H. Roberts discovered a scrap of papyrus in Egypt containing portions of 18:31-33, 37, 38 that disproved their theory. This fragment, the Rylands papyrus, was written around A.D. 125. "**

I tease, but...if I picked up 2,000 year old paper and wrote something on it with 1,000 year old ink, written in the style of Homer from 3,000 years ago, how old does that make the text?

Huh?

Now, I don't care about Roberts or the papyrus. What was that first part?

A.D. 170? Whoa! When I picked up my first Bible in third grade, and began to flip through my RSV, the sequence of the books of the Bible implied that Genesis was first and Revelation was last, right? Alpha and Omega.

Suddenly, the error in my assumption became clear.

First, Revelation was written around 95 AD

Then, the Epistles were written during the second century.

Lastly, John wrote his Gospel?

Wow, it suddenly made sense. The Rylands debate seemed irrelevant. Whether 125 or 170, John would have been DANG old. Miraculously old, right?

So with this in mind, I tried to re-read the text, and to also see if there was anything else out there to support this idea.

Guess what?

## Back to Eusebius

Remember our researcher? Well, the Council of Nicaea happened in the year 325 AD. Eusebius, the Bishop of Caesarea, was born in 265 AD. If the scholars in the 18th century had been right, that would have meant John wrote the Gospel only 95 years before our researcher was born.

Eusebius obviously never met John, or else he wouldn't have included what Polycrates wrote to Victor. Yet in preparing the History of the Church, he dug up every nugget he deemed valuable. In it, he bridges the authenticity of John through two degrees of separation through Christian writers like Polycarp (directly trained by John) and Irenaeus (trained by Polycarp), who was quoted by Eusebius.

While modern scholars can split hairs, Eusebius was VERY CLOSE to the time period, wasn't he? While he gave me all sorts of insights about the life of John not included in the Bible, here is the insight that really opened my eyes (Book 3, Chapter 24:

**"Let us now point out the undisputed writings of this apostle. And in the first place his Gospel, which is known to all the churches under heaven, must be acknowledged as genuine. That it has with good reason been put by the ancients in the fourth place, after the other three Gospels, may be made evident in the following way."**

So the first detail that caught my attention is that John wrote his account AFTER the other three Gospels came into existence. Christendom was already reading these three Gospels before he'd touched pen to paper. Eusebius also said they didn't write the Gospels right away because, you know, they thought they had to orally spread the Gospels.

**"Nevertheless, of all the disciples of the Lord, only Matthew and John have left us written memorials, and they, tradition says, were led to write only under the pressure of necessity. For Matthew, who had at first preached to the Hebrews, when he was about to go to other peoples, committed his Gospel to writing in his native tongue, and thus compensated those whom he was obliged to leave for the loss of his presence. And when Mark and Luke had already published their Gospels, they say that John, who had employed all his**

time in proclaiming the Gospel orally, finally proceeded to write for the following reason."

Notice how Eusebius points out that Mathew's was the most "Hebrew" since it was written in his native tongue, which explains some strange things like Hebrew time given during the Easter story while John will use "Roman" times. Remember, if Jerusalem was wiped out in 70 AD, John did not have much of a Hebrew audience, did he?

**"The three Gospels already mentioned having come into the hands of all and into his own too, they say that he accepted them and bore witness to their truthfulness;"**

**"They say, therefore, that the apostle John, being asked to do it for this reason, gave in his Gospel an account of the period which had been omitted by the earlier evangelists,"**

John gave his stamp of approval. How cool is that? Now, if he not only began the "canon" of New Testament texts, notice his motivation for why he wrote it—things omitted. He wasn't saying Luke was wrong or Matthew messed something up; John had been there. He knew the dates for everything. He knew what happened first, second, third, etc.

So picture him with all three texts open, flipping through each of them, and seeing when they skipped important moments. For this reason, John specifically gives holidays and day-by-day mentions so he can frame what the others have written. He resists the temptation to revise or edit. Instead, he writes his own account, pinning the vague moments in Luke to specific times found in his own account.

Again, young third grade Jason locked the mental sequences into his mind BEFORE he read John, who clarifies all three Gospels. Read them again, with John as the framework. It's quite different. Because of this, John steps in only when necessary, pointing out when something happened, and adding moments he felt should have been included. If the other three got something right, he skipped it in his own account. Yet his account is the most chronological, even if he skips over important moments.

**"And the genealogy of our Savior according to the flesh John quite naturally omitted, because it had been already given by Matthew and Luke, and began with the doctrine of his divinity, which had, as it were, been reserved for him, as their superior, by the divine Spirit. These things may suffice, which we have said concerning the Gospel of John."**

Having done my own study of all four gospels, I arrived at some different conclusions than Eusebius, but the theory about John writing his own Gospel AFTER the others certainly opened my mind.

**"But of the writings of John, not only his Gospel, but also the former of his epistles, has been accepted without dispute both now and in ancient times. But the other two are disputed. In regard to the Apocalypse, the opinions of most men are still divided. But at the proper time this question likewise shall be decided from the testimony of the ancients"**

While Eusebius never says whether 125 AD or 170 AD is when John wrote the Gospel, it helped me realize that the issues made by scholars might have a plausible explanation.

## A Bit of Hindsight

Having read my "Witness Theory," I'd like you to now take it to the end. At the age of 75, John immediately wrote down the Revelation and delivered it to the Seven Churches and began a program of recruiting rugged evangelists (who are tough enough to become criminals). During this period, he was still just JOHN, which is how he addressed himself in the text.

Later, he wrote letters to a young church, threatened by Gnostics. Since it is now the second century, he is still looking 75 but inside, he is well over a hundred. Writing from this older perspective, and beginning to believe Jesus is going to make him **tarry** until he returns, John sees the young Christian church as "little children."

Finally, he sits down, years prior to the Council of Nicaea, and realizes that spreading the Gospels to all nations might take a bit. To help, he gathers the written works of his peers, including Matthew, Mark, and Luke, and gives his stamp of approval so that his rugged evangelists can distribute these texts.

Oh, hey, wait a moment. Let me write mine also.

So when John prepares to write his Gospel in the mid second century, he is a different man than the one who walked with Christ. He's learned from Peter and Mary, been arrested and boiled in oil, visited by angels and Christ at Patmos, spread the Revelation, addressed Gnosticism, and saved the soul of a robber. And he's also REALLY old. With this in mind, he takes a deep breath and begins his account as a wise old man.

**Old Guy Perspective #1—The Word.**

He begins with an eternal view of Christ, not a biographical account. He knows from Revelation 12 the full story of Christ, and thus, begins with a Cosmic view of things, including a reference to "the Darkness," a possible foe for him in the End Times.

**Old Guy Perspective #2—Wedding at Cana.**

He clarifies that Jesus's ministry began at the Baptism (to which he witnessed). Having read MML, he inserts a trip to Cana, which includes an End Times Bride/Groom metaphor he now understands better.

**Old Guy Perspective #3—Other Disciples.**

His clarification places this before the Temptation in the Wilderness and brings Jesus back to Jerusalem for an initial interaction with money changers, Nicodemus, and a gathering of his Judean disciples (guys like Judas and Thomas) BEFORE he returns to find the Galilean crew fishing.

**Old Guy Perspective #4—Missed messages.**

John not only gives time context to Luke's chaotic, random accounts but he amplifies with his "big picture" philosophies that the others didn't include.

**Old Guy Perspective #5—The Promise.**

John must have sighed when he read both accounts of the martyr promise, which he didn't bother correcting or justifying.

**Old Guy Perspective #6—Lazarus.**

What a scene. Not only does it define the power over death of Christ, but it also foreshadows a moment with Mary Magdalene at the tomb.

**Old Guy Perspective #7—Anointing of Feet.**

Speaking of Mary Magdalene, John DOES correct the other writers, by placing the scene into the Passover Festival timeline, including how the sacrificial lamb is supposed to be cleaned before being brought into the house. Six Days prior...it mattered to John.

**Old Guy Perspective #8—Yep, it's me.**

John adds a strange little detail in 13:23, where Christ reveals to "the disciple whom Jesus loved" that Judas was the Son of Perdition. Good to know if you're the witness, right?

**Old Guy Perspective #9—The final sermon.**

Now, Luke does a nice job with his Gospel, but why was the goodbye speech ignored? Well, Peter (Luke's source) had a rough night that night, didn't he? Years later, John sees the "big picture" speech about the future of Christendom too insightful not to include. In a way, it is Christ's goodbye to all of us waiting for his return.

**Old Guy Perspective #10—Fixing Easter.**

John was the guy who knew the Passover regulations so well that Jesus let him prepare the Last Supper. Decades later, John splits hairs down to the hour about when things happened. Remember, most Christians are not Jewish at the time he writes his Gospel, so his account explains the hours in Roman time, clarifying the vague Hebrew night/day and hours. If you read it closely enough, you'll see a completely different timeline based on John's subtle inclusion of things like "Preparation Day of the Passover," "Lamb Day," "Feast," and "Preparation Day" to help a non-Hebrew reader (like yours truly) understand the timeline better.

Thanks, John.

## Old Guy Perspective #11—Glory Days.

While all four Gospels sprinkle together the details for Easter morning, John adds a funny detail—he's faster than Peter (knee slapper).

## Old Guy Perspective #12—Peter.

Remember the breakfast by the sea?

Told you we would get back to this. For John, it has been a long, long time since he's seen his friend and mentor, Peter, who was killed decades earlier in Rome. Decades after it happened, John remembered this poignant scene:

> **[John 21:18] Verily, verily, I say unto thee, When thou wast young, thou girdedst thyself, and walkedst whither thou wouldest: but when thou shalt be old, thou shalt stretch forth thy hands, and another shall gird thee, and carry thee whither thou wouldest not. [19] This spake he, signifying by what death he should glorify God.**

Peter died, and now, only John remained. For this reason, I believe John identifies himself as the Beloved Disciple. Back then, he and Peter were almost rivals. It's not that he won and Peter lost, but John now understands what purpose Christ had for him. He was going to be "set aside" so he could be one of the Two Witnesses, dying the best martyr's death possible. Decades after being told about it, John no longer sees himself by name but as by title, which is why as an old guy, he never uses his name. There is no ego left...only the love of Christ. He has become the Beloved Disciple

**[John 21:20] Then Peter, turning about, seeth the disciple whom Jesus loved following; which also leaned on his breast at supper, and said, Lord, which is he that betrayeth thee? [21] Peter seeing him saith to Jesus, Lord, and what shall this man do? [22] Jesus saith unto him, If I will that he tarry till I come, what is that to thee? follow thou me.**

Now, we've been over this part quite a few times, haven't we, but now, as we picture John finishing his Gospel, ask yourself why he finishes with this anecdote.

Not only does he connect himself to the "Beloved Disciple" title, but he brings up what Jesus said, which is a line about remaining until Jesus comes again. Look where John goes next...

**[23] Then went this saying abroad among the brethren, that that disciple should not die: yet Jesus said not unto him, He shall not die; but, If I will that he tarry till I come, what is that to thee?**

Ya think, John? You're freaking everybody out. Why are you still alive in the second century? John comes right out and addresses the elephant in the room that confused 18th century scholars. How can John be the author of the Gospel when all manuscripts appear to come from the second century?

Apparently, in John's circle of second century friends, they thought he was an immortal. Coyly, John addresses them by clarifying that he's not immortal because Jesus promised him a good death, a witness's death, one day in Jerusalem. Pithy, John. Very pithy.

**[24] This is the disciple which testifieth of these things, and wrote these things: and we know that his testimony is true. [25] And there are also many other things which Jesus did, the which, if they should be written every one, I suppose that even**

**the world itself could not contain the books that should be written.**

Yes, little children, it's John, the Son of Thunder, the Beloved Disciple, who not only writes this Gospel but will also one day stand as a witness in Jerusalem to this and all the other things that cannot be contained in a book.

Alas, this is all that I could contain in this book. I hope you enjoyed this out of the box look at the Beloved Disciple. I hope I'm right, but I certainly could be wrong, so examine scripture and decide for yourself. As my researching buddy Eusebius wrote: **"But at the proper time this question likewise shall be decided."**

Indeed.

Oh, almost forgot…

**[John 21:25] "Amen."**

## ABOUT THE AUTHOR

Jason Lee Willis, a self-described Luth-olic-a-tist, characterizes himself as "just a nerd with a Bible" and has led adult and youth small group studies at home and at church for the past three decades. As a former English teacher who explored literature to find possibilities rather than absolute answers, Willis looks for "out of the box" interpretations with a preference for the most "epic" answers. While versed in world mythology and history, he remains the son of the church secretary raised in a conservative small town.

## ALSO BY JASON LEE WILLIS
Examining the Seven Kings
Examining Moses
Examining Christmas
Examining Gospel Timelines

www.ingramcontent.com/pod-product-compliance
Lightning Source LLC
Chambersburg PA
CBHW061757120626
46550CB00005B/2024